NASHVILLE
HAUNTED HANDBOOK

AMERICA'S
HAUNTED ROAD TRIP

TITLES IN THE AMERICA'S HAUNTED ROAD TRIP SERIES:

NASHVILLE
HAUNTED HANDBOOK

**jeff morris, garett merk,
and donna marsh**

clerisy press

Nashville Haunted Handbook

For further information, contact the publisher at:
Clerisy Press
P.O. Box 8874
Cincinnati, OH 45208-0874
www.clerisypress.com

Library of Congress Cataloging-in-Publication Data
  Morris, Jeff, 1978-
    Nashville haunted handbook / By Jeff Morris, Garett Merk, and Donna Marsh. — 1st ed.
        p. cm. -- (America's haunted road trip)
    ISBN-13: 978-1-57860-497-5
    ISBN-10: 1-57860-497-4
    1. Haunted places—Tennessee—Nashville. I. Merk, Garett. II. Marsh, Donna
        (Donna L.) III. Title.
    BF1472.U6M685 2011
    133.109768'55--dc23
                                        2011022282

Distributed by Publishers Group West
Printed in the United States of America
First edition, first printing

Editor: Lady Vowell Smith
Cover design by Scott McGrew
Text design by Annie Long
Cover and interior photos provided by the authors unless otherwise noted.

CONTENTS

SECTION I   cemeteries   3

SECTION II   historic houses   33

SECTION III bars and restaurants   75

SECTION IV stores and hotels   113

SECTION V roads and parks 143

SECTION VI miscellaneous 187

ACKNOWLEDGMENTS

WE WOULD LIKE TO START BY THANKING all of those nameless people out there who made this book possible. During our countless hours of research into this vast array of haunted locations, we were helped by so many people who either wished to remain anonymous or whose name we never knew. It almost seems unfair that many of the people who helped us the most may not be individually named in this section. For this reason, we feel that these people should be mentioned first. You have our most sincere apology for not including your name, and you have our most sincere thank-you.

Next, there are a handful of people who assisted with the daunting amount of research that was necessary for this book. Without these people, this book would not have been possible: Nicole Dunn, Chris Smith, Lawrence Michaels, Michele Carter, Johnny Cash, Jerry Zoeller, Matt Kroeger, Michael Lamping, Stephanie Ollech, James Nash, Alan Brown, Joanne Shelton, Richard Edgeworth, Dudley Pitts, Terry Mayo, and Brad Zeltmer.

Many individual stories throughout this book can be credited to individuals who helped us obtain the stories and history of the locations. Joe Peters, owner of the Walking Horse Hotel, thank you for telling us stories and allowing us to investigate your amazing hotel. Adam Russell, thank you for helping us track down the ghostly happenings at Hume-Fogg High School. Yvonne Clark, thank you for both your encouragement and the amazing research that you did to help us along the way.

Another person who made this book possible is Ryan Vehr. Ryan was indispensible during our many excursions into the city of Nashville. He helped to discover and photograph several of the locations that appear in the book. He did this selflessly, sacrificing his own time and money to help us. He deserves credit for some of the photographs in this book, and he deserves our gratitude for his contributions.

Next, we would like to thank our friends at the American Paranormal Society: Monica Leister, Fran Staley, Tanya Green, Wayne and Judy Meeker, Carol Humphrey, Scott and Neth Williams, Nikki Nelson-Hicks, Melanie Nelson, David and Nicholle Rockwell, Heather Beckwith, and Ron and Chris Noel. These people all deserve a very special mention because they are responsible for many of the locations that are featured in this book. They are true paranormal explorers and researchers who helped us discover many of the haunted sites described in the following pages.

Finally, we would all like to individually extend thanks to family and to people who have helped us along the way:

DONNA: My sons, Jonathan Dyer and Jordan Marsh, deserve a tremendous thank-you for all of the hours they spent with me going through cemeteries, researching sites, and poring over evidence when I'm sure they would rather have been hanging out with their friends. And my parents, Randall and Shirley McCormick, have my gratitude for encouraging me to go for it.

JEFF: My wife, Amy, my son, Koen, and my stepdaughter, Dakota, deserve my gratitude. Not only did they sacrifice their own time to pick up the slack at home while I worked on this book, but they also encouraged me and pushed me to be my best. My parents also deserve my thanks. Their encouragement helped to get me through all those long hours of writing and research. Finally, my brother, Mike, who helped me with the *Cincinnati Haunted Handbook*, deserves my thanks. He has been my partner throughout my career as a writer. Without him, I never would have made it to this point.

GARETT: I'd like to thank my parents and God for making me; without such I couldn't have helped write this book. I'd like to thank my family for being supportive; ghosts for existing (without them this book would make no sense); Garfield for being awesome; my truck for getting us to and from Nashville; the Nashville Predators fans for making one of our trips more interesting; and Elvis Presley, because without him I would not now have an awesome picture of me and a statue of him.

FOREWORD

WHEN I CAME UP WITH THE IDEA for the *Haunted Handbook* series, I started by looking toward many of the other ghost books that were already out there. I have always loved reading ghost stories, and these stories were always so much better when they were supposedly true. My favorite ghost books were the ones that had some sort of documented history behind the ghosts. I wanted to know why these ghosts were there, what happened on a certain road that gave rise to the ghosts that now reside there, or who was buried in a certain cemetery that caused it to be haunted. I also enjoyed knowing where the haunted locations were and how to get to them. As great as I thought these books were, I always had the belief that with enough research and hard work, I could make a better guide.

The first thing I set out to improve was the fact that the other ghost books out there usually left me wanting more. My favorite ghost books told anywhere from 17 to 34 ghost stories apiece about as many haunted locations. While these stories were sometimes terrifying and always interesting, I was always left wondering why the books stopped at so few of them. It seemed that there were so many more stories out there, and I wanted to hear them all.

When I set out to create the first *Haunted Handbook*, based in my hometown of Cincinnati, my goal was to include an unprecedented number of ghost stories in the book. It all started when I told my publisher that I was pretty sure I could get 50 haunted locations in a single book. Soon that changed to 75, and then to 90. Once I was confident that I could find ghost stories for 90 different haunted locations, I convinced myself that a hundred locations was possible. Instead of simply including a handful of haunted sites, we were ultimately able to include 100 places. In my opinion, the sheer number of locations is one of the most interesting facets of this series.

The next thing that I felt needed to be addressed in the *Haunted Handbook* series is the geographical focus. Many of my favorite ghost books focused on too wide an area, some even including stories from all across the country. Others had stories from across an entire state. I would always find myself skimming through these books, looking for those locations that I was able to recognize or that were close enough to me that I could go visit an actual haunted location. Unfortunately, many times this meant that only two or three locations in each book would really pique my interest.

The *Haunted Handbook* series addresses this issue by making sure that all 100 locations in the book are within an hour's drive of the center of the city. This means that if you live in that city, whether you were aware that they were haunted or not, you are probably familiar with most of the locations. Tourists can visit any of the locations with the knowledge that they are never too far away from their hotel. Instead of having to flip through the book looking for those sites that are close, readers can now read through each chapter, knowing that each location is nearby.

The final thing that I wished my favorite ghost books would talk about is how to go looking for these ghosts. I have always liked to pretend that I was an explorer. I would rather learn about some haunted location and then go out and visit the place. The books that inspired me to start writing my own ghost books would capture my interest about a certain cemetery or haunted road, but I would have no idea how to get to the location or when the place closed. I would often wonder if it was okay to go there at night or if a certain place was safe to visit alone.

I decided to add sections that I hoped would answer these questions for the reader. Included with every chapter are both a section giving directions to each location and a section describing how to visit it if you were going there with the intention of looking for ghosts. Also, in lieu of a map in every section, I added the address, allowing readers to plug that information into a GPS unit before setting off on their adventures. All this helps make the book accessible to both those people who read ghost books only to get scared in the safety of their own home and those paranormal explorers who want to go out and find these ghosts for themselves.

As we move forward to the *Nashville Haunted Handbook*, the series has done nothing but progress. There are several appendixes that have been added to the Nashville guide that weren't included in the Cincinnati book. We've invited new authors and experts to help create this book. Donna Marsh is an author from Nashville and the founder of the American Paranormal Society, which is based in middle Tennessee, and Garett Merk is an author and founder of Tri-State Paranormal and Oddities Observation Practitioners, which is based in southwestern Ohio.

This book was incredibly fun to help create, and I was glad to have been a part of it. I was amazed by how eclectic the ghost stories are in Nashville. I learned more than

I ever thought possible about both the Civil War and country music. The locations that I had the most fun with, though, were the strange places unique to the area. There is a llama in White Bluff that roams the forests and eats children. There is an antiques store in Lebanon with an electric chair and a "genuine" bigfoot head. A grave in downtown Nashville is made from the actual cliffside where a woman leapt to her death. These stories make the mummy that comes to life and ravages a local museum every once in a while seem almost normal.

I hope that you enjoy reading this book as much as we enjoyed writing it. Go ahead, go out and explore the strange paranormal side of Nashville, Tennessee.

Enjoy!

Jeff

INTRODUCTION

TALES OF GHOSTS AND HAUNTINGS have fascinated me for as long as I can remember. As a child I devoured every book I could find in the local library, staying up late in order to sneak in just one more thrill before bed. However, I craved more as an adult so I became a paranormal investigator. It was the perfect way to indulge my passion for the supernatural.

When I moved to Nashville in 1997, I wasn't sure if I could continue to indulge my interest or not because there just didn't seem to be many books or much information about the ghosts of Music City. I joined a local ghost-hunting group and hoped for the best. Nashville didn't disappoint me.

Dreams produce passion, passion produces energy, and that energy imprints itself on the surrounding area. Nashville is a city of dreams and passions. It was occupied during the Civil War, is the site of the nation's worst train accident, gave birth to more number-one records than I can count, and so much more. The first white settlers came here with dreams of a new life, and people still do that today—only today's dreams are quite often of making it big in the music industry.

With such a history is it any wonder that Nashville is a city full of ghosts? From haunted battlefields to spooky honky-tonks to long-forgotten tunnels, Nashville has it all, and I've been lucky enough to visit and even investigate some of Music City's most haunted spots. Now, with the publication of *Nashville Haunted Handbook*, you can visit some of these sites as well.

Nashville Haunted Handbook gives you not only the history and ghost story for each location but also directions to the site, as well as little hints and tidbits to make your visit a success. All that is asked is that you hunt both safely and respectfully. Remember, it's not the dead you have to fear but the living, so always practice safe ghost hunting by letting someone know where you're heading and when you can be expected to return.

Also, hunt respectfully. Your actions reflect on other ghost enthusiasts, so always leave a site better than you found it—clean up a bit, pick up garbage, and treat the site as if it were your very own. Don't do anything you wouldn't want someone to do to your final resting spot.

But enough of Mom's lecture. Enjoy this book, enjoy the sites, and please let us know if you find any evidence of ghostly activity. We'd love to hear about it. Contact us on Facebook at www.facebook.com/nashville.haunted.handbook.

Happy Hunting!

Donna L. Marsh

SECTION I

cemeteries

BLUE SPRING CEMETERY

1529 Middle Blue Springs Rd., Ashland City, TN 37015

directions

Stay on I-24 West from downtown Nashville for about 18 miles to exit 31, the New Hope Road exit. Turn left onto New Hope Road and follow the road for a little more than a mile and a half to Old Clarksville Pike. Turn right onto Old Clarksville Pike and follow that for a little less than a mile before turning left onto Bear Wallow Road. Follow Bear Wallow for almost a mile and a half, and then turn right onto Peter Pond Road. Follow Peter Pond Road for a half mile, and then turn right to stay on Peter Pond Road. Continue to follow Peter Pond for about 2 miles. You will then make a sharp left onto Carney Winters Road/Middle Blue Springs Road. The cemetery will be on the right just past the intersection. The cemetery is visible from the road.

history

This cemetery is located in a remote section of Ashland City and is rather far from any businesses or public places. The cemetery is surrounded by two houses that were eventually built around it. The property lines of these houses border the fence that surrounds the small cemetery.

The history of the cemetery itself is rather unremarkable. There are some children who were buried here, which is not unusual for a cemetery that has been around since the 1800s when children would die more frequently. There are many more adults than children buried in the cemetery, though. While each person buried here is likely to have his or her own interesting story, those stories are left for the ghosts to tell.

ghost story

Most of the ghosts of this cemetery show themselves when people are either driving by on the adjacent road or when people park their cars on the adjacent road and look into the cemetery. People who park their cars on the road will often hear a car approaching. As they wait for the car to arrive, the sound slowly fades away. There are no places where this ghostly car could have turned off the road.

People also will often see shadowy figures walking through the cemetery at night. When these figures are investigated, there is never any sign of them anywhere in the cemetery. The gate to the cemetery is secure, and there is no place where the figures could have left.

The most famous ghost of this cemetery, however, is that of a small girl who walks the cemetery at night. This girl will appear as a white glowing apparition that is either sitting on a small bench within the cemetery near a small statue of a girl or walking around near the same bench. When the girl is spotted, she will suddenly look up at the frightened witness and vanish.

visiting

Even though the cemetery is off limits at night, you can still experience these ghosts after the sun sets. The cemetery is quite small and its entirety is visible from a small parking area alongside the adjacent road. You can park your car there in the middle of the night and watch the cemetery for shadowy figures even though the cemetery itself is closed. As long as you don't walk onto the property of the abutting houses or cross the fence into the cemetery itself, you are not trespassing, and you can watch the haunted cemetery for apparitions to your heart's content.

CEDAR GROVE CEMETERY
609 South Maple St., Lebanon, TN 37087

directions
Take I-40 East for 28 miles to Exit 238, US 231 South toward Lebanon. Turn left onto US 231 South. Follow this road for a mile before turning left onto West Adams Avenue. Turn left onto South Maple Street. Cedar Grove will be the cemetery on your left. The cemetery on your right is another one called Memorial Cemetery that is not reputed to be haunted.

history
Even though Cedar Grove Cemetery has been the city cemetery of Lebanon, Tennessee, since 1823, it wasn't at its current location until it was moved from the churchyard of the College Street Church of Christ in 1846. Many of the important men from the area are buried here in this cemetery, including a Confederate general, a Tennessee governor, and a Supreme Court chief justice.

The cemetery itself also contains more than 130 Confederate soldiers who died during the war or were veterans who died later. The cemetery remains in use and is still growing. The cemetery land encompasses 34.6 acres, but at this point only 23 acres are being used for burials.

ghost story

There is only one ghost story reported here at Cedar Grove, but this story is repeated quite often. At night, when gazing into the cemetery from outside its gates, people will often see strange lights moving throughout the cemetery. Many times these lights will be purple and white and will float among the headstones quickly.

Oftentimes people will see these lights out of the corner of their eyes and then will look closer to find that the lights have vanished. Other times, people will see the lights clearly and they will slowly float throughout the cemetery. These lights will look almost like distant lanterns being carried by some unseen spirits.

visiting

It is difficult to describe the rules for visiting this cemetery. First of all, the ghosts here are lights, so the only time that you can experience these ghosts is after dark. Many of the sightings have been made by people who are on the adjacent street. These witnesses will see the lights from the public road and will watch them in fascination until they vanish.

Watching the lights from the street is probably the best way to experience these ghosts, but there is another way. This cemetery does not close. The cemetery staff would prefer that everyone stay out of the cemetery after dark, but officially, the cemetery is open throughout the night. We believe that it is just as easy to experience these ghosts from outside the cemetery gates as it is within, but if you see something strange inside and want to take a closer look, it is not illegal to enter the cemetery.

There is also a candlelight tour of the cemetery every October. The tour does not tell any ghost stories or encourage ghosts in any way, but it is a guided tour of the cemetery after dark that does focus on the more famous grave sites.

DYER CEMETERY

8538 Dyer Rd., Rockvale, TN 37153

directions

Take I-24 East for about 23 miles to Exit 74A, TN 840 West toward Franklin. Follow this road for a little more than 2 miles to Exit 50 toward Beesley Road, and then turn left at the end of the exit ramp onto Veterans Parkway. After another 2 miles, turn right onto Franklin Road. Take your second left onto Kingwood Lane. Follow Kingwood for another 2.5 miles before turning right onto Windrow Road. Follow Windrow for 3 miles before angling right onto South Windrow Road. After another mile, turn right onto Dyer Road. The cemetery is near the end of Dyer Road.

history

When they needed a place to bury their loved ones, a family in this remote area with the last name of Dyer established the Dyer Cemetery in the early 1800s. Since this property was somewhat remote, it made sense for them to create their family's cemetery on the grounds. Eventually the cemetery fell into the care of the Leathers family who lived nearby. The Leathers family cares for the cemetery today.

A strange story circulates about the cemetery. The story takes place in the 1800s, but it is unclear whether the events occurred before or after the Dyer family started using the land as their own. What happened was that three women in a nearby town were accused of being witches and of conspiring with Satan. They fled the town but were followed by a lynch mob to what was or what would become the Dyers' property. Eventually the witches were cornered, and the mob hung the witches from a tree and then burned their bodies. Their charred remains were buried where the cemetery is today.

ghost story

Victims of the ghosts here are most often initially approached at the front gate. Due to the terrain and the condition of the gate itself, it is difficult to push open in order to enter the cemetery. Many times, though, people who are struggling to open the gate will have it suddenly fling open for no apparent reason.

Once inside the gate, there is no lack of ghostly activity. Visitors will encounter shadowy figures that approach quickly and maliciously and then vanish. Footsteps will approach people in the dark of the cemetery, but no one will be there. Most of this activity will occur near the rear of the cemetery.

In the front of the cemetery, a cedar tree is rumored to have been the tree where the witches were hung. Near this tree, people will feel a hand grab an arm or shoulder but then turn around and find no one there. Others will feel scratches that resemble either fingernails or straw running down an arm. Sometimes, balls of fire will appear near the tree and will slowly ascend the tree and then disappear. If the story of the witches is actually true, the ghosts seem to be quite upset.

visiting

Unfortunately, in order to see the ghosts here you will have to go at night. The strange behavior of the front gate, the shadowy figures, the balls of fire, and the sounds have been exclusively reported after nightfall. From what we can tell, it seems that the cemetery is open after dark. If you do go there at night, make certain that you search for any signs along the road or at the front gate that suggest that the cemetery closes at dusk. These rules are always subject to change, so even if the cemetery is open all night now, that rule may change tomorrow.

Also, keep in mind that this cemetery is rather remote. Make sure to keep your safety in mind at all times. Don't go alone. And don't approach the shadowy figures; they may just be real people up to no good.

EVERGREEN CEMETERY

519 Greenland Dr., Murfreesboro, TN 37130

directions

Evergreen Cemetery is in Murfreesboro near the battlefield. From downtown Nashville, take I-24 East for about 27 miles to Exit 78B. Take Exit 78B toward Murfreesboro on the Old Fort Parkway. After 3 miles on Old Fort Parkway, turn right onto Clark Boulevard; then take your third right onto North Highland Avenue. The entrance to the cemetery will be your third left on Highland.

history

This cemetery wasn't established until 1872, making it strange at first sight that the most famous feature of the cemetery is a circle of Confederate dead. The story of the Confederate Circle in Evergreen Cemetery starts at the Battle of Murfreesboro (see the Slaughter Pen at Stones River National Battlefield chapter) during the Civil War. Thousands of men from both sides of the battle were killed during the brutal fighting. Many of the Confederate dead were buried at the Old Confederate Cemetery, a mile and a half south of Murfreesboro across the street from the Samsonite luggage plant.

In 1891, it was determined that the bodies of the Confederate dead be moved to Evergreen Cemetery within the city of Murfreesboro itself. Over 2,000 bodies were moved from the mass grave at the Old Confederate Cemetery to the Confederate Circle at Evergreen.

ghost story

The Confederate dead roam Evergreen Cemetery to this day. There are many different stories of encounters with these soldiers here. Most often, people will report seeing actual shadowy figures walking through the cemetery in the vicinity of the Confederate Circle at night. Sometimes, these figures are wearing Civil War uniforms. Since the figures are only silhouettes when they are seen, it is impossible to tell if the uniforms are gray or blue, but witnesses report that the ghosts are in Civil War uniforms.

Other witnesses report feelings of uneasiness near the Confederate Circle. People feel as if they are being watched or followed through the cemetery. Other people will hear the distant sounds of battle or will hear moans coming from the ground. These phenomena are experienced during both day and night.

visiting

Evergreen Cemetery closes at dusk, so do not attempt to enter the cemetery after this time. The cemetery is visible from outside the walls, so you can walk the perimeter of the cemetery after dark looking for the shadowy figures that are said to roam here. Other ghostly phenomena, though, have been reported during the day in the vicinity of the Confederate Circle. Feel free to stroll the cemetery during the day listening for the sounds that have haunted this site since the Confederate dead were moved here in 1891.

FOREST LAWN MEMORIAL GARDENS

1150 South Dickerson Rd., Goodlettsville, TN 37072

directions

North of Nashville in a small town called Goodlettsville sits Forest Lawn Memorial Gardens. To get there, simply take I-65 North for about 6.5 miles to Exit 90A, the Dickerson Pike exit. Take a right onto Dickerson Pike and follow the road for about 5 miles. The cemetery will be on the right-hand side of the road. It is the only large cemetery in the area. You can't miss it.

history

Unlike many of the other cemeteries in the area, Forest Lawn does not have a remarkably long history. In fact, this cemetery did not accept its first burial until 1954, only a little more than 50 years ago. This doesn't mean that Forest Lawn does not have its own bit of history to share with anyone who is listening.

The most interesting part of this cemetery is a section known as Music Row, named after the Music Row district in downtown Nashville, mostly because many of the people buried in this section are country music legends. Many died suddenly and tragically while still in their prime.

On a rainy night in 1963, Patsy Cline was flying home from a show with several country music stars. The weather got the best of the plane, and it went down near Camden, Tennessee, instantly killing all on board. Lloyd Copas, Hawkshaw Hawkins, and Randy Hughes were all killed in the accident and were then buried at Forest Lawn.

On his way to the memorial service for Patsy Cline, country music star Jack Anglin was driving alone and took a corner too quickly. He lost control of the vehicle and crashed. He died and was buried at Forest Lawn as well.

ghost story

This cemetery itself does not seem to be haunted at all. It actually looks quite peaceful and beautiful. The fact that nothing appears to be creepy or ominous throughout the entire cemetery makes it all the more surprising when reports surface about strange things that happen here.

No one has ever seen a ghost at Forest Lawn Memorial Gardens. The ghosts here do seem to have something to say, though. Witnesses will sometimes hear what sounds like distant music when they walk near the Music Row section of the cemetery. Other times people will feel uncomfortable when walking alone near this section.

The most common occurrence at this cemetery, however, is that amateur ghosthunters with audio recorders will often record strange voices that they didn't experience at the time of the recording. This "electronic voice phenomenon" seems quite prevalent here at Forest Lawn. People will record anything from whispers to music that wasn't heard at the time the recording was made.

visiting

Normally, the best time to search for the Forest Lawn ghosts is during the day since the cemetery closes at dusk and the ghost stories here require you to actually enter its confines. This is OK, however, because most of the reports and recordings that originated here were made during daylight hours. Be respectful, bring a recorder, and explore the cemetery. Make sure you spend most of your time in the Music Row section since this is where most of the reports come from.

GRAVE OF GRANNY WHITE

Travelers Ridge Drive and Granny White Pike,
Nashville, TN 37220

directions

This strange location is about 5 miles outside of downtown Nashville. Simply take
12th Avenue South from the city. After a couple miles, the road changes its name to
Granny White Pike. Follow the same road for another 2.5 to 3 miles until you see
Travelers Ridge Drive on your left by the sign that says "Inns of Granny White." The
grave itself is fenced off at the front of the subdivision.

history

Early in 1743, nearly 270 years ago, Granny White was born in North Carolina. Her
early life was quite normal for a woman from that area and time. She married a man
named Zachariah, had children, and lived happily. Things began to change when her
husband was killed at the Battle of the Bluffs in 1781. Granny White, then named
Lucy White, was left without money. Things compounded when her son died, leaving
her two grandchildren, Thomas and Willis, orphaned. In 1801, the State of North

Carolina declared that she was unfit to care for her two grandchildren, so she took them with her and moved to Tennessee, settling on the land where the Inns of Granny White sit today.

In order to make enough money to care for her small family, she used the culinary skills that she had developed earlier in her life. She set up an inn and a restaurant that quickly became popular with the weary men who had just traversed the Natchez Trace, which ended four miles from her property. Her ingenuity and business savvy allowed her and her grandchildren to survive. Granny White eventually passed away in 1816 and was buried on her property. The nearby road leading into Nashville was named after her.

ghost story

The spirit of Granny White lives on despite the fact that she has been dead for almost 200 years. While her memory may have inspired many older people never to give up, in a more literal sense people have encountered the actual spirit of Granny White even today.

The story goes that if you were to approach the grave of Granny White at any time of the day or night, you will experience this ghost. Her ghost takes the form of a simple sound. If you stand near the grave, you will supposedly be able to hear the sound of a heartbeat coming from the ground. Sometimes, if you're standing close enough, you can even feel that beating heart through the ground. Granny White's story speaks of an unwillingness to give up despite age and adversity. Perhaps her will still hasn't given out and her heart continues to beat audibly to this day.

visiting

The grave itself is fenced off, but you can still walk close enough to experience its unique ghost. This area near the grave where the ghostly heartbeat can be heard does not close at night. If you want to experience the added creepiness of approaching the grave after dark, there is nothing to stop you from doing so.

This doesn't mean that the ghostly heartbeat will only manifest at night. You are more than able to approach the grave during the day as well. Just stand there for a few moments being as still as you can. Most people who try this will eventually hear the sounds of her heart still beating beneath the ground.

HENDERSONVILLE MEMORY GARDENS

353 East Main St., Hendersonville, TN 37075

directions

Take I-65 North for 12 miles to Exit 95, the Vietnam Veterans Boulevard exit. Follow Vietnam Veterans Boulevard for about 7 miles to Exit 7, Callender Lane. At the end of the exit ramp, turn right onto Indian Lake Boulevard. Follow Indian Lake for almost a mile, and then turn left onto North Anderson Lane. Follow this road for a little more than half a mile, and then turn left onto East Main Street. The Hendersonville Memory Gardens are in the Woodlawn Cemetery, which will be on your right just after the turn.

history

Younger cemeteries are rarely reputed to be haunted, but there are always exceptions. This cemetery has been around for only about 50 years and has been called Hendersonville Memory Gardens for an even shorter time. The cemetery was originally known as Woodlawn Memorial Park East, but its name was changed in 2003 to Hendersonville Memory Gardens.

Some of the more famous country music stars in Nashville are buried in this cemetery. June Carter Cash, the beloved wife of Johnny Cash, was buried here in

2003 when she died of cancer. Crushed by the death of his wife, Johnny Cash died later that same year and was buried next to her.

ghost story

It is no wonder that Johnny Cash who was called the "Man in Black" in life would retain that moniker even after death. On the same note, is it really any wonder that people have seen a man in black roaming through this particular cemetery at dusk?

The ghost story that is repeated most often here is that people will see a man dressed in a black suit walking along the sidewalk beside Johnny Cash's grave. When people glimpse this man in black, they are typically across the cemetery and just happen to glance up to see him. When they go to investigate, there is no sign of the man.

visiting

The cemetery itself closes at dusk, so you are unable to enter after dark. Johnny Cash's grave site lies at the highest point in the cemetery, so it is visible from almost anywhere else on the grounds. At night, though, it would be impossible to see a figure on the hill from outside the gates, especially if he were dressed in black.

Your best bet for encountering the ghost of Johnny Cash is to enter the cemetery during regular visiting hours and go to an area across the cemetery from the Cash grave. This is where people typically are when they see the man in black.

McGAVOCK CONFEDERATE CEMETERY

1345 Carnton Ln., Franklin, TN 37064

directions

Exit downtown by taking TN 6 South/US 31 South/8th Avenue South/US 70 Scenic East, and continue to follow this road for the next 18 miles. When you reach the traffic circle, continue straight onto Main Street and then turn left onto 5th Avenue South. Follow 5th Avenue slightly to the right as it becomes Lewisburg Avenue. A little more than half a mile down the road, turn right onto Carnton Lane. The cemetery is across the parking lot from the mansion and gardens.

history

After the brutal night of the Battle of Franklin in November 1864, dead and wounded Confederate soldiers littered the entire city of Franklin. The larger houses in the area were used as hospitals, and Carnton Plantation was no exception (see Carnton Plantation chapter). When the house filled up with the wounded, the dying were laid upon the mansion's grounds. Hundreds died in and around the house.

John and Carrie McGavock, the owners of the plantation, donated the two acres abutting their family cemetery to bury the Confederate dead. Due to the large number of dead that had to be buried there, the Confederate Cemetery at Carnton (also called the McGavock Confederate Cemetery) is the largest privately owned military cemetery in the country.

ghost story

Both the McGavock Family Cemetery and the Confederate Cemetery here at Carnton are reputed to be haunted. Most of the time, the ghosts are described simply as strange sounds which rise from within the gates of the cemetery. Moans and sighs will often be heard. It will sound as if someone is writhing in pain here in the cemetery, even when it is empty.

There are three other ghosts that haunt this particular cemetery. If you were to enter the Confederate Cemetery from the family cemetery side, in one of the rows on the right twin brothers are buried directly beside one another. Many times when people are walking past the graves of these twins, they will feel something rub against their ankle. Occasionally they will actually feel a hand grab their ankle.

The other ghost here is perhaps the most famous one. A ghost of a little girl walks both the Confederate Cemetery and the family cemetery immediately adjacent. The little girl will always be seen walking or running up and down the fence, pulling a stick across the metal bars. Sometimes the little girl isn't seen at all but people will still hear the sounds of a stick hitting each bar of the fence.

visiting

Going into this cemetery after dark is illegal. The property is open from 9 a.m. to 5 p.m. every day of the week except Sunday when it is open from 1 to 5 p.m. The cemetery is free to visit during these hours. Since the grounds are closed at all other times, the only time to explore the cemetery and look for these ghosts is during its open daytime hours. Luckily, this is when the reports of the ghosts commonly occur.

MOUNTOLIVETCEMETERY

1101 Lebanon Pike, Nashville, TN 37210

directions

Head out of downtown by taking I-40 East toward Knoxville. Take Exit 212, the Fessler's Lane exit, and keep left at the fork until you find yourself on Rundle Avenue. Turn left onto Fessler's Lane. After a half mile, turn right onto Lebanon Pike. Mount Olivet Cemetery will be on your right.

history

Mount Olivet Cemetery is the final resting place of many of central Tennessee's most prominent politicians. Several former governors of Tennessee have been laid to rest here since it opened in 1856, and many other senators and congressmen have been buried within its borders. The cemetery has quickly established itself as one of the more prominent cemeteries in the Nashville area.

In the years following the Civil War, Southerners came together and organized a movement to bury many of the Confederate dead in prominent cemeteries in major cities in the South. Mount Olivet became one of those cemeteries that would house these fallen southern soldiers. More than 1,500 Confederate dead are buried in the Confederate Circle area at Mount Olivet.

ghost story

While among the paranormal community, orbs (balls of light that float around haunted places without any apparent cause in photographs and video) have generally been discounted as being light reflections off of bugs or dust, many people still cannot explain the strange balls of light that appear in photos and video taken within this particular cemetery. People will often walk through the cemetery snapping photos, not realizing anything is amiss, but upon later reviewing the pictures they discover many strange, inexplicable balls of light.

Yet these orbs are just the tip of the proverbial paranormal iceberg here at Mount Olivet. Many of the stories here involve strange disembodied voices that travel throughout the cemetery at night. The voices will be very loud and strong. It will almost sound as if a deceased politician is orating from beyond the grave within the 250-acre cemetery.

Still another ghost walks the grounds of this cemetery at dusk and throughout the night. People will often see a dark shadow that walks throughout the headstones, only to suddenly disappear. The apparition seems to replay the same motions night after night, walking from the Confederate Circle and disappearing into the darkness of the cemetery, and then later returning to the Confederate Circle and vanishing into thin air.

visiting

It is unfortunate that this cemetery closes at dusk. This makes it difficult but not impossible to experience many of the ghostly happenings here. Photographs from outside the gates will still supply the photographer with mysterious balls of light. While many of these orbs are probably bugs or dust, it is impossible to tell which ones may actually be paranormal.

The strong voices of the politicians are audible from outside the gates as well, making these ghostly voices easy to experience. Perhaps the most difficult phenomenon to witness here is unfortunately the most famous. It is difficult to see the Confederate Circle from beyond the gate, and this is the area where the shadowy specter is seen most often. Your best bet to experience this ghost is to be in the cemetery at dusk as the sun begins to set. People will often see the ghost at this time of day as well, and it is not illegal to be within the cemetery's walls.

OLD BEECH CEMETERY

3216 Long Hollow Pike, Hendersonville, TN 37075

directions

Take I-65 North until you reach Exit 97, the Long Hollow Pike exit toward Goodlettsville. At the end of the exit, turn right onto Long Hollow Pike. Follow Long Hollow Pike for about 6 miles. The Old Beech Cemetery will be on your left in the churchyard of the Beech Cumberland Presbyterian Church. If you reach Buccaneer Boulevard, you've gone too far.

history

This cemetery and the adjacent church are the oldest remaining cemetery and church in Hendersonville. The church was founded in 1798, and its original founder is buried in the cemetery. There are older graves here, dating back to the days of the Revolutionary War.

The church itself suffered fires twice during its long existence. No one was killed during these fires, but the building itself was very important to all who worshipped there. Many of the church's worshippers over the years have been buried in this cemetery, and many of these people are likely to be the reason for its ghosts.

ghost story

Generally the ghosts at the Old Beech Cemetery only come out at night. This is because the most prolific ghosts here are ghost lights. When the ghost lights appear in the cemetery, they always emerge in pairs and put on a show for those here to witness them. The lights will seem to chase each other through the cemetery for several minutes at a time. Whenever anyone enters the cemetery to search for the source of these strange lights, nothing is ever found.

Others have reported seeing shadowy figures walking through the cemetery at night or have reported feeling uncomfortable when walking through the cemetery at any time. There have been accounts of voices coming from the cemetery as well. These voices are audible, and they are almost always preceded by a sudden drop in temperature.

visiting

Old Beech is another cemetery that is closed after dark. This is unfortunate since many of the ghost stories here occur exclusively at night. If you are set on trying to find the nighttime ghosts here, the parking lot for the adjacent church is your best bet. Simply park in the lot and watch the cemetery for playful lights. Just don't enter the grounds of the cemetery after it closes.

Many of the voices or intangible feelings will occur at any time of the day when the cemetery is still open to the public. These ghosts are easier to experience.

OLD CITY CEMETERY: BOULDER TOMBSTONE

1001 Fourth Ave. South, Nashville, TN 37210

directions

Old City Cemetery, also known as Nashville City Cemetery, which holds the boulder tombstone, is just south of downtown on Fourth Avenue. Facing the river on Broadway, turn right onto Fourth Avenue and follow it for about a mile until you pass I-40. The cemetery is just past Oak Street. The boulder is a huge tombstone near the main building at the center that cannot be missed. The name on the boulder is Ann Rawlins Sanders, 1815–1836.

history

Here at the boulder tombstone, there are known truths and then there are legends that may or may not be true. We know that the person whose name is on the stone, Ann Sanders, was 21 at the time of her death, that she married Charles Sanders four years before her death, and that she died at midnight on March 30, 1836.

The stories behind her death are less verifiable since, in the early 1800s, if someone committed suicide it wasn't widely advertised. The story goes that in March of 1836, Ann and Charles got into a huge lover's quarrel. At the climax of the quarrel, Ann ran away, not sure about the fate of her marriage or what would become of her. Depressed, she found her way to a cliff overlooking the Cumberland River and looked down into the water below. Feeling that she had nothing left to live for, she jumped into the river and drowned.

Charles repented after the fight and went looking for her. Eventually, he discovered what had happened and was completely crushed. In order to mark her grave, he had a chunk of rock removed from the cliff where she jumped. It was used to mark her grave in the city cemetery. Ann was afraid of the dark, so in order to make sure that she was comfortable in death, Charles attached a lantern to the top of the stone. Since then, the stone has gained the nickname "Suicide Rock."

ghost story

You would not be surprised to find out that the ghost stories that involve this tombstone seem to match aspects of the legend that accompanies the stone. Most of the stories involve sounds that happen at any time during the day or night. Witnesses will often hear sobbing coming from near the boulder even though there is no one else around. When they stand near the boulder, people will also hear arguments that sound as if they are coming from a distance. Perhaps these are echoes of the final lover's quarrel that cost Ann her life.

There are other ghosts that haunt the area as well. Sometimes the lantern above the boulder appears to be lit in the middle of the night although the cemetery is closed and no one has been there to light it. Other times, people will see a figure of a man in period clothing approaching the stone and reaching up toward the lantern as if to light it. People will also see a young woman standing atop the stone with a sad look upon her face. The woman vanishes when approached.

visiting

No one can enter this cemetery after dark. It is only open until 4 p.m. throughout the year. This does not make it impossible to experience the ghosts here, however. The sounds are heard at all hours, so you can go during the cemetery's open hours to experience these ghostly sounds. The lighting of the lantern at night can be experienced from the public road after dark. Just make sure you don't enter the cemetery after it closes or you may be fined for trespassing.

OLD HENDERSONVILLE CEMETERY

115 Walton Ferry Rd., Hendersonville, TN 37075

directions

Take I-65 North for 12 miles to Exit 95, the Vietnam Veterans Boulevard exit toward Hendersonville/Gallatin. Follow this road for 3 miles to Exit 3 to the Johnny Cash Parkway toward Hendersonville. Follow this road for a little more than 3 miles, and then turn right onto Walton Ferry Road. The cemetery is not easy to find. It is actually hidden behind a strip mall on your left, on a small strip of grass between the Roma Pizza & Pasta restaurant and the loading dock for the grocery store.

history

For the last few decades, cemeteries in general have gotten larger. While at first it may seem that the growth of cemeteries may have something to do with the increase in population, it may also be the result of the speed of travel. The deceased can be moved farther distances nowadays and loved ones can travel farther distances in order to regularly visit them. The days of burying loved ones on your own property are all but gone. While the days of small cemeteries have almost passed, many such cemeteries remain scattered throughout the country. For many of these cemeteries, records were never kept and a lot of the history has been lost.

This small cemetery, nestled in Hendersonville behind a grocery store and a strip mall, has been around since the 1800s. The dates on the headstones also show that many of the people buried here were children. While the stones do not describe what could have caused so many children to be buried within so small a place, many afflictions from the 1800s and early 1900s, such as cholera, tended to smite the young.

ghost story

Young people, cut down before they have ever had a chance to really experience life, will typically create ghosts. The ghosts at this cemetery are most often seen by the people who run the shops in the nearby strip mall. Since the cemetery is hidden behind the mall, those who regularly have reason to walk out behind the buildings are often the only ones who are even aware that the cemetery is there. The ghost that is most often seen at the cemetery is that of a little girl. When the witnesses see the girl, they generally report that she is dressed in white and is running around the cemetery as if she is playing. As quickly as she appears in the cemetery, she suddenly vanishes.

The little girl is not always seen wearing white; she is sometimes seen in a pinafore dress. The girl in the pinafore acts similarly to the girl in white, but since there are so many children buried in the cemetery and she is wearing something different, some witnesses feel that there are two different spirits who haunt the cemetery.

Beyond the two little girls, witnesses will also encounter balls of light floating through the cemetery and shadowy figures walking around and through the small cemetery. Ghost investigators who have entered the cemetery with audio equipment have captured phantom voices on their recordings.

visiting

Exploring this cemetery at night is legal. At this time, there are no signs or rules that suggest that this cemetery, like many others, closes at dusk. This would make a search for shadow figures or balls of light much easier.

RESTHAVEN MEMORIAL GARDENS

2930 US 41A, Clarksville, TN 37043

directions

In order to get to Resthaven Memorial Gardens, take I-24 West for 25 miles to Exit 19. Turn left on TN 256 South. After about a half mile, turn right onto US 41A. Follow this road for about 9 miles. The cemetery will be on your left just past Miller Road.

history

There was once a plantation house that sat just behind the cemetery's current location, and the plantation itself encompassed much of the cemetery land. Many slaves worked on the plantation and the owner was known for being quite harsh on them. Nothing was tolerated here.

The plantation owner's daughter ended up falling in love with one of the slaves, and they secretly carried on an affair on the grounds for quite some time. This all ended, though, when the owner's daughter became pregnant. She withheld it from her father as long as she could, but eventually she began to show her pregnancy. In a fit of rage, her father demanded she tell him what happened. Terrified of what her father would do to her, she told him that she was raped by a slave. The father found the slave and brutally murdered him.

ghost story

The grounds of the cemetery are haunted. Many of the ghosts seem to be remnants of those people who are buried here. Visitors will often see dark shadowy figures walking throughout the cemetery that mysteriously vanish when approached.

Other witnesses to the paranormal will actually see the ghost of the slave who was brutally killed on the grounds of the cemetery. He is seen roaming the grounds, supposedly looking for his lost child.

Many times, the ghosts here are seen in the dead of night. Strange lights, which look like white or green lanterns, may be seen floating throughout the grounds of the cemetery. Many people who see these lights will be suddenly approached by them and will drive away from the scene in terror. Those who flee from these lights will often have rocks thrown at their cars.

visiting

Open only during daylight hours, you are unable to actually enter this cemetery after nightfall. This doesn't make it impossible to experience the ghosts here, however. The cemetery is boxed in by two public roads, US 41A and Miller Road. You can drive up and down these roads or even stop your car on these roads near the cemetery at night and gaze into the cemetery looking for figures or lights.

Some of the ghosts are even seen during the day as well. You can certainly enter the cemetery at any time during regular hours and try to experience the ghosts here.

WOODLAWN MEMORIAL PARK CEMETERY

660 Thompson Lane, Nashville, TN 37204

directions

Take I-65 South for about 4 miles to Exit 79, the Armory Drive exit. Merge onto Armory Drive and follow the road for about a mile. Take a left onto Sidco Drive and follow this road for a little more than half a mile. Turn left onto Thompson Lane. The cemetery will be on both your right and left just after the turn. Since the cemetery is surrounding you, it is hard to miss. There is a large sign at the main entrance.

history

Ghosts seem unlikely at Woodlawn given its natural and tranquil appearance. If you delve deeper into the area's history, though, many facets of this place give this cemetery a unique, darker tinge.

During the Civil War, battles raged nearby and many of the wounded from the battles were taken to a building which still stands within the cemetery grounds. This building was used as a hospital, and many soldiers suffered and died within it. Today, the building still stands, surrounded by bouquets of flowers and a small duck pond.

For almost half a decade after the Civil War, the Lignon family used the property as farmland until they decided that the land could be better used as a cemetery. Since the cemeteries that were closer to the city were quickly filling up, the Lignons decided that they would create a cemetery here on the outskirts of town and make its appearance original enough to attract new business. In 1900, instead of creating the usual cemetery of the time with upright headstones, the Lignons decided that they would lay grave markers flat on the ground. To this end, the beauty of the landscape would be the defining feature instead of the headstones themselves. The cemetery attracted plenty of business and has been in operation for more than 100 years.

ghost story

No one would guess that this peaceful and tranquil landscape has its own collection of ghost stories. Most of these ghosts seem to congregate around the Civil War–era hospital which still stands on the grounds of the cemetery. Often, people will see shadowy figures out of the corner of their eye near the building. These figures will appear and then disappear so quickly that the witnesses may wonder if they are a figment of the imagination or if there was anything actually there. Other times, people will hear what sounds like distant weeping coming from the vicinity of the old hospital. When these sounds are investigated, the source is never found.

Another strange thing that visitors report is that the eyes of the few statues throughout the cemetery seem to follow them as they walk by. The statues are not memorials to individual people but decorations positioned throughout the site. Perhaps they are sentinels, watching the living carefully to make sure they don't step out of line.

visiting

The cemetery closes at dusk. This is OK if you are going to the cemetery, hoping that one of the statues will watch you as you pass. This phenomenon often happens in the middle of the day, so you can enter the cemetery when it is open and see if the statues are watching you.

The shadowy figures and sounds are a little harder to experience. These are mostly reported at dusk or at night after the cemetery has closed. Since the cemetery closes at dusk, that time frame just before the sun dips below the horizon is your best chance of encountering these ghosts.

Resthaven Memorial Gardens, see page 28

SECTION II

historic houses

BELLE MEADE PLANTATION
5025 Harding Pike, Nashville, TN 37205

directions
Take I-40 West to I-440 East. Follow I-440 East for a little more than a mile to Exit 1A, US 70 South/ TN 1 West. Follow this road for a little more than 3.5 miles. The Belle Meade Plantation will be on your left.

history
Early in the plantation's history, several modest buildings served as living quarters before the mansion was completed in 1853. In 1848, the nine-month-old daughter of the plantation's owner, William Harding, fell ill inside one of these buildings. Despite all the care that the doting parents attempted to shower upon the ailing child, the baby died.

Despite the death of the child, the plantation itself prospered until war came to the area in the early 1860s. Fighting during the Civil War actually occurred in the front yard of the mansion. Today, evidence of this fighting is still visible in the bullet holes that riddle the home's front columns.

In 1953, the mansion was given to the Association for the Preservation of Tennessee Antiquities and has operated as a museum ever since.

ghost story

Hints of the tragedies that have occurred throughout this plantation's many years seem to still exist throughout the property. Many people have heard what sounds like a child crying in the building even when there are no children anywhere nearby. The crying sounds distant. Those who hear it aren't entirely sure they actually heard anything at all. They think that maybe it is a trick of the mind until the people that they are with report hearing the exact same thing.

There are motion sensors throughout the building that often go off for supernatural reasons. For a week in 1987, the motion sensors went off five of seven nights at almost the exact same time, between 3:40 and 3:47 a.m. When the authorities showed up to confront the trespassers, the building was secure and there was absolutely no one or nothing inside.

Other witnesses to the paranormal will hear footsteps in the hallways and sometimes what sounds like a woman giggling. Despite the fact that some have died here in the building, someone or something seems to be living on.

visiting

The only way for a visitor to experience the ghosts here at Belle Meade is to take a tour of the mansion during its regular hours. The mansion is open for tours from 9 a.m. to 5 p.m. every day, and admission is $16. The building is an excellent example of a Nashville plantation from the mid-1800s and is well worth visiting, especially since there is a chance you may meet one of the resident ghosts. If you don't want to pay the money for the tour but still want to see the building, you are out of luck. They actually charge you to walk the grounds of the mansion as well. If you want to get a glimpse of a ghost here, be prepared to pay.

BELMONT MANSION

1900 Belmont Blvd., Nashville, TN 37212

directions

Near downtown, you can get to the Belmont Mansion from the heart of the city in less than 15 minutes. Simply take Broadway out to 12th Avenue South to Ashwood Avenue. Turn right onto Ashwood Avenue. Almost a half mile down Ashwood, take a left onto Belmont Boulevard. The mansion is on the Belmont University campus and will be on your left.

history

The mansion itself dates back to 1853, and throughout the years of its existence, it has seen its share of pain and drama. Most people believe that the ghost who walks these halls is the ghost of Adelicia Acklen.

Ms. Acklen was known to be quite good at manipulating men, and she used this skill to her advantage often, eventually becoming one of the wealthiest women in post–Civil War Nashville. While most people from the South were impoverished to some extent during the years just after the war, Adelicia flourished and flaunted her wealth without reservation.

Despite her financial luck, she did meet with her own share of personal heartache. Several of her children succumbed to disease and died in the house at very young ages. This completely devastated Adelicia, and she would withdraw from society for long periods of time after each death. Often, it would take her months to emerge from her depression.

During the latter years of her life, Adelicia would often comment to guests that "you can't take it with you." In 1887, Adelicia herself died in the mansion. Today, the mansion is the largest house museum in Tennessee and the only such house whose history centers upon the life of a woman.

ghost story

It seems that Adelicia is attempting to defy her own adage and has indeed taken her grand mansion with her into the afterlife—or perhaps she just never left in the first place. All of the activity in this house can be attributed to Adelicia's ghost.

Most of the ghostly sightings here actually involve a full-figured apparition of Adelicia herself. People will see a woman dressed in a lavish mid-1800s dress walking the halls of Belmont. People will see her all throughout the mansion. Sometimes she is glimpsed at the end of a long hallway before she immediately vanishes. Other times she is seen standing by the windows in upstairs rooms. Once, a woman visitor was walking down a hallway in the building and turned a corner, only to find herself face-to-face with the ghost of Adelicia. Turning around and fleeing in terror, the witness didn't wait to give the apparition a chance to vanish.

Some say that Adelicia stays at the mansion, waiting for her deceased children to return to her. Others claim that she loved her life and her home so much that she was unwilling to leave. Everyone who has seen the ghost believes that it is Adelicia herself, as permanent a fixture in the area as the house.

visiting

The mansion is closed to the public at night. But this doesn't mean that it is impossible for you to encounter the ghost of Adelicia Acklen. The mansion itself is a museum, and it is open for tours during the day all throughout the week. From Monday through Saturday, the museum is open from 10 a.m. to 4 p.m., and on Sunday it is open from 1 p.m. to 4 p.m. Guided tours move throughout the house during the day and take about 45 minutes to an hour. These tours are your best chance to explore the building and perhaps catch a glimpse of the famous ghost. Admission to the mansion does cost $10 for adults, but even if you do not catch sight of the ghost, it is well worth the money to see the historic mansion itself.

BUCHANAN LOG HOUSE

2910 Elm Hill Pike, Nashville, TN 37214

directions

Nine miles from downtown, the Buchanan Log House sits alongside a busy suburban road. Take I-40 East for about 8 miles to Exit 216C, the Donelson Pike exit. Turn right onto Donelson Pike, and travel for a little more than a half mile. Turn right onto Elm Hill Pike, and follow it for a little more than a half mile. The home will be on the left-hand side of the road. There is a historic marker and a sign by a wooden fence next to the driveway for the log house.

history

This building is one of the older standing structures in the state of Tennessee, having been built in 1809. In 1811, James Buchanan, the builder of the cabin, married Lucinda East, and they began to build a life in the house.

Less than 10 years after they married, James and Lucinda already had 16 children, and the small three-room house did not have nearly enough space to accommodate the family's growing needs. James then built an extension onto the house in 1820 to help house his large family.

In 1841, James Buchanan died at the age of 78 and was buried across the street at the Buchanan Cemetery. His epitaph concludes with the rather ominous line, "Prepare to die and follow me." Twenty-four years later, Lucinda's mortal remains did follow James to the cemetery across the street. Some say that her spirit stayed with the house.

ghost story

It seems that this small log house is still occupied by the ghost of Lucinda East Buchanan. The ghost itself is rarely encountered by anyone who is actually living in the house or visiting but is instead reported by people who are driving by on the adjacent road.

Passersby will report seeing a woman dressed in period clothing sitting on the front porch of the log house. While the rustic and historic appearance of the house does not make the woman look out of place, there is no reason that someone dressed like this would be sitting there. Other witnesses will see a woman dressed in period clothing in the windows of the building, watching the yard and the nearby road.

visiting

It is not a difficult prospect to visit the ghost here at the Buchanan Log House since many of the ghost stories are reported when the witnesses are outside of the house. Driving down the adjacent road and looking up at the house may be your best bet because this is how most of the sightings happen, but the road itself is rather far from the house, and it is very difficult to see the windows from the road. There is a small parking area next to the building where you can park and watch the outside of the house as long as you do so during the day. All of the sightings of Lucinda have occurred during daylight hours.

The building is available for tours on a limited basis. You can call for an appointment to take a tour or you can visit the home on Tuesday or Friday before 4 p.m. during spring, winter, and fall.

CARNTON PLANTATION

1345 Carnton Lane, Franklin, TN 37064

directions

From downtown, take TN 6 South/US 31 South/8th Avenue South/US 70 Scenic East, and continue to follow this road for the next 18 miles. When you reach the traffic circle, continue straight onto Main Street and then turn left onto 5th Avenue South. Follow 5th Avenue slightly to the right as it becomes Lewisburg Avenue. A little more than half a mile down the road, turn right onto Carnton Lane. The plantation and house will be on your left.

history

Important people from across the country would come to Carnton after it was built in 1826. A former mayor of Nashville named Randal McGavock built the house as an important social destination for politicians of the time, including President Andrew

Jackson. However, tragedy and heartache would eventually seep into the once idyllic ambience of the plantation and completely change its atmosphere.

When Randal died in 1843, Carnton passed to his son, John. John and his wife, Carrie, had five children, but three of those children died in the house at a young age, a tragedy that would forever affect John, Carrie, and the entire atmosphere of the house.

Eventually, death would enter this household in a much more dramatic way. On November 30, 1864, the Battle of Franklin raged throughout the night. The dying and wounded were moved to local buildings for medical care, and since Carnton was such a large house so close to the epicenter of the battle (see Carter House chapter), Carnton became the largest field hospital in the area. Estimates suggest that at least 300 Confederate wounded and dying were in the house at any given time. Beyond this, the grounds and slave quarters were also used to tend to the dead. Hundreds of Confederate soldiers died on this property in the aftermath of the battle. Today, you can still see the bloodstains on the floors throughout the house, most markedly within the children's bedroom, which was used as an operating room.

Land adjacent to the family cemetery on the property was used to bury nearly 1,500 Confederate dead in the aftermath of the battle (see McGavock Confederate Cemetery chapter). Within the next few decades, the house and the Confederate cemetery would both fall somewhat into disrepair. It wasn't until relatively recently that the house and cemetery were restored and turned into the museum that it is today.

ghost story

Nearly every corner of this property is said to contain ghosts, most likely because of the somewhat dark history here. The first ghost that is often seen and heard within the house itself has been named by those who witness her "the Weeping Maiden." People will see a woman dressed in Civil War–era clothing crying in different areas of the house. The bottom quarter of her dress is always soaked with blood. Sometimes, this weeping maiden is not seen but is simply heard, her sobs echoing through the house without any discernible source.

Another ghost that resides in this house is a fiddler that haunts the front parlor. Again, this ghost is both seen and heard by employees and visitors alike.

Once, the final group tour of the day was visiting the upstairs of the building after the house had been locked up for the night. To their surprise, they saw a woman and a small boy in Civil War clothing walking back and forth across the balcony. Suddenly these two figures vanished. On another occasion, a boy tried to climb the railing on the same balcony but was noticeably pushed off by some unseen force.

Finally, there are many ghostly remnants here from the Battle of Franklin. Voices of dying soldiers can be heard throughout the property. Also, the sounds of battle itself can often be detected in the distance by visitors to Carnton Plantation.

visiting

For normal tours, the building is open from 9 a.m. to 5 p.m. every day of the week except Sunday, when it's open from 1 to 5 p.m. These tours are a good time to experience many of the ghosts at the plantation because this is when many of the sightings occur. Tours last for an hour and cost $12 per person. The last tour starts at 4 p.m.

During the Halloween season, Carnton also offers ghost tours of the property at night. The cost of the tour is $20, and the tour times and dates are subject to change. For further information about the ghost tours, visit the building's website at www.carnton.org.

CARTER HOUSE

1140 Columbia Ave., Franklin, TN 37064

directions

From downtown Nashville, take I-65 South to Exit 74B, merging onto TN 254 West/ Old Hickory Boulevard toward Brentwood. Turn left at Franklin Pike and continue onto TN 6 South/US 31 South/Franklin Road. Continue straight at the traffic circle onto Main Street/Public Square, continuing to follow Main Street. Take a left onto Columbia Avenue, and the Carter House is on the right.

history

Essentially, the Carter House was the epicenter of one of the bloodiest battles of the entire Civil War. The house itself was built in 1829 by a man named Fountain Carter, and for many years his family lived in the house in relative happiness. Eventually, Fountain's wife died in the house along with 4 of his 12 children. When the Civil War broke out, three of Fountain's sons joined the Confederate army.

One of these sons, Tod Carter, became captain. He was captured at Missionary Ridge but escaped, returning to his unit to continue the fight. Since he had gone through the hardships of being a prisoner of war, his unit allowed him to go visit his family in Franklin.

On the night of November 29, Tod stayed the night at a friend's house, which was only a couple miles from his family home. He planned to reunite with his family the next day. History would have other plans. Union forces had planned to sneak past the Confederate forces in Franklin by crossing the Harpeth River during the night. Unfortunately, the river level was too high and the Union forces could not cross. They set up defenses at the Carter home and braced for the next day's attack.

It wasn't until around 4 p.m. the next day that the Confederate forces were finally organized enough to mount an attack. The battle raged through most of the night. Tod Carter, knowing that his family was trapped inside the house that stood at the center of the battle, organized a charge toward the Union center and his family home. He was hit by several bullets and fell in his own yard.

The Confederate army won the battle but lost almost three times as many men as the Union. Tod, wounded, was carried into the Carter House, where he was laid on

the bed in his sister Annie's room. He died from his wounds only a couple feet from the place where he was born.

ghost story

Nearly 150 years has passed since the Battle of Franklin, but the ghosts of that night are still prevalent within the home. While there are, of course, ghostly remnants of soldiers here who died during the battle, either manifested through phantom footsteps or inexplicable shadows, the most often experienced casualty of the battle is that of Tod Carter himself. Tod can be seen throughout the house, most often sitting on the side of the bed in Annie's room where he died or in the hallway in the downstairs of the house. It seems as if Tod finally made it home and nothing—not even death—is going to take him away.

Much of the other phenomena that occur here are attributed to Annie Carter, Tod's sister. Items will suddenly move by themselves, falling inexplicably from a dresser or simply flying as if tossed across the room. Other times, a ball will roll down the hallway without anyone having pushed it, or an unsuspecting tourist will feel a tug on his or her sleeve, only to look down and find no one there.

Occasionally, people will hear the voice of a friendly woman welcoming them to the house despite the fact that there is no one there.

visiting

Since most of the activity here at the Carter House actually occurs within the home itself, you will probably need to enter the building during regular business hours in order to experience the ghosts. The building itself is open for tours from 9:30 a.m. to 5 p.m. every day of the week, and tours cost $12 a person. The grounds of the house are included on the tour, so you are unable to explore the grounds and the battlefield unless you pay admission.

At 5 p.m., the building and grounds close to the public, so if you want to experience some of the ghostly activity here, it would have to be before the house closes. Luckily, though, a lot of the activity here does happen during the day, and you may just get that chance to encounter one of these spirits.

CLOVER BOTTOM MANSION

2941 Lebanon Rd., Nashville, TN 37243

directions

Take I-40 East for about 6 miles to the Briley Parkway exit, Exit 215B. Follow this road for about 2 miles to the Lebanon Pike exit, Exit 8. Turn right onto Lebanon Pike, and follow the road for a little more than 2 miles. The Clover Bottom Mansion will be on your right.

history

Easily one of the largest plantations in the Nashville area, Clover Bottom was constructed in 1854 by a man named Dr. James Hoggatt. Only two years after its original construction, a tragic fire hit the mansion and did extensive damage to it. When reconstructing the building, Hoggatt decided to give the façade a more original and artistic appearance that it originally had. The Italianate style of today's building was added to the mansion after the fire in 1856.

The plantation did quite well, and at one point more than 60 slaves worked on the extensive property. Eventually, Dr. Hoggatt contracted a disease that slowly wasted him away. He died in the house after a long bout with the mysterious illness.

ghost story

The ghosts that inhabit the Clover Bottom Mansion tend to haunt the building by making sounds. Most of these sounds come in the form of footsteps. Generally these footsteps will be clearly audible even though the people who hear them are certain that they are the only living people within the building.

Many of these footsteps sound very distinctly from a different time period. When downstairs in the house, people will hear the sound of wooden-heeled shoes clicking against the wood floor overhead. The upstairs is accessible only to staff, and even when no staff members are supposedly upstairs, these footsteps are still clearly heard. People will also sometimes hear the sounds of rustling skirts throughout the house, even when there are no women wearing skirts anywhere nearby.

visiting

Entering the downstairs of this building is easy. It is free to tour the downstairs of the building mostly because it is not set up as any kind of museum but rather serves as the offices of the Tennessee Historical Commission. If you want a historic tour of a magnificent mansion, you will be disappointed if you go to Clover Bottom Mansion; but if you want to visit a haunted historic mansion to listen for ghostly footsteps, you couldn't ask for a better price of admission than free.

CRAGFONT

200 Cragfont Rd., Castalian Springs, TN 37031

directions

Exit downtown Nashville by taking I-65 North for about 11 miles to Exit 95. Take Exit 95, TN 386 North toward Hendersonville/Gallatin. Take TN 386 for 16 miles, and then turn right onto the entrance ramp to TN 109 South. Follow TN 109 for about 7 miles, and then turn right onto Hartsville Pike. After another 3.5 miles, turn left onto Cragfont Road. The Cragfont mansion will be on your right.

history

The original Cragfont home was built in 1785 and was a simple log cabin on a high bluff. It was built by two men, James and George Winchester, who were important figures in the early history of Tennessee. George was eventually killed by Native Americans in nearby Gallatin, leaving James the property. James decided to build an opulent mansion on the site of the original cabin.

By 1802, the mansion was completed and was considered by many to be the grandest home west of the Appalachian Mountains. James was involved in Tennessee politics, becoming the speaker of the Tennessee senate at one point in his career. The house itself would host many of the most important people in Tennessee, such as Andrew Jackson and Sam Houston.

James Winchester died in the house in 1826, but the house stayed with the family until the death of James's wife, Susan, in 1864. The home switched owners several times before the State of Tennessee purchased the house in 1958 and opened it to the public.

ghost story

Many strange things happen at the Cragfont mansion. Most of the time, these strange events occur after the building has been locked up for the night. Caretakers will often return to the building after it has been closed, only to find things very different from the way they were left the night before. Furniture will be moved to different places throughout the rooms. Beds that were neatly made the previous night will appear to have been slept in during the night. Candles that were unlit the night before will be lit when the building is opened in the morning.

Activity has also been reported during visiting hours. People will see full-figured apparitions and hear footsteps throughout the house. When these apparitions and sounds are investigated, the source is never found. Objects have also been thrown across rooms at people, scaring them out of the house.

visiting

You are typically not able to enter the building during the winter. From November through mid-April, Cragfont closes and only opens by special appointment. Throughout the rest of the year, the building is open to the public for tours Tuesday through Saturday from 10 a.m. to 5 p.m., and Sunday from 1 p.m. to 5 p.m. During regular visiting hours, the price of admission is only $5.

Unfortunately, the only way to really encounter the ghosts here is to enter the building itself, and the only way to do this is to go during the part of the year that the building is open. If you do have a chance to visit the building, it is well worth the $5. You stand a chance of experiencing not only some ghostly activity here, but also an important piece of Tennessee history.

THE HERMITAGE

4580 Rachel's Lane, Hermitage, TN 37076

directions

The Hermitage is located approximately 12 miles east of downtown Nashville. Take I-40 East to Exit 221A (The Hermitage exit). Follow the highway around and continue on Old Hickory Boulevard until you see the sign for The Hermitage on your right.

history

In 1791, Rachel Robards met Andrew Jackson, future president of the United States, and they almost instantly fell in love. The problem was that Rachel was still married to her estranged husband Lewis Robards. Until 1794, Rachel and Andrew lived as if they were married but were impeded by the fact that she was still married to someone else. Finally, in 1794, she divorced, and she became Rachel Jackson.

In the early 1800s, Andrew and Rachel moved to the property where The Hermitage stands today, originally living in a two-story log cabin from which they ran their plantation. By the end of 1820, the mansion was finally ready and Rachel loved it. She put everything she had into its design and decoration.

Their happy life began to collapse during the presidential election of 1828, when Andrew Jackson ran for a second time. His opponent, John Quincy Adams, mounted personal attacks against Jackson, calling Rachel a whore and a bigamist since she was still married when she and Andrew started seeing each other. This destroyed Rachel, and Andrew attributed her death on December 22, 1828, to the stress she suffered from these attacks.

Crushed by her death, he endured a presidency filled with personal turmoil and regret. On top of this, the Hermitage mansion that Rachel had worked so hard on was gutted by fire in 1834. When Jackson returned from the presidency, he made sure that the mansion was restored to its state before the fire, the state that Rachel had worked so hard to perfect. Andrew Jackson died in a downstairs bedroom of the house in 1845.

ghost story

Excited about having purchased the property to restore it, some of the ladies of the historical society decided to spend the night in the house. They brought a mattress from one of the upstairs bedrooms down to the front parlor and settled in for the night. After midnight, they were awakened by the sounds of pots, pans, and dishes being thrown around the kitchen. This was followed by what sounded like heavy chains being dragged across the front porch. When they looked out the window, they saw nothing. Not long after that, they heard the sounds of someone riding a horse up and down the stairs. A thorough check of the mansion turned up nothing, and they spent a sleepless night. They stayed the next night as well and were again treated to the spectral show. After that, The Hermitage was entrusted to a guard.

Since then, many other hauntings have been reported throughout the property. People will often see apparitions of slaves on the grounds, especially on the wooded trail that runs past the old slave quarters and the plantation fields. Disembodied voices are also heard from time to time, both inside the mansion and throughout the rest of the property. On occasion, full apparitions of early 19th-century people have been seen and even photographed within the house.

visiting

It is against the rules to take photographs inside the house. However, there are apparitions and ghostly phenomena reported all throughout the grounds, and the remainder of the property is open to photograph and explore.

The Hermitage has operated continuously as a museum since 1889, and it is open daily from 8:30 a.m. to 5 p.m. from April 1 to October 15, and 9 a.m. to 4:30 p.m. from October 16 to March 31. It is closed Thanksgiving, Christmas, and the third week in January. Be sure to allow at least two hours for the tour.

LOTZ HOUSE

1111 Columbia Ave., Franklin, TN 37064

directions

Take I-65 South to Exit 65 toward Franklin. Turn right onto Murfreesboro Road and follow the road for about 2.5 miles. Turn left onto Church Street and then, less than a half mile down the road, turn left again onto Columbia Avenue. The Lotz House will be the white building on the left with a cannon in the front.

history

In 1858, the house itself was built by a German immigrant named Johann Lotz who designed many of its unique features. The house's true fate and importance would not come into being until November 1864, when the Battle of Franklin erupted during the night.

When the Union soldiers dug in around the Lotz House, the family fled to the Carters' house across the street (see the Carter House chapter). In the short and bloody battle, hundreds of soldiers died in and around the Lotz home. Immediately following the battle, the Lotz House was used as a hospital and continued as a hospital throughout the rest of the war. Hundreds more would die within the house because the medical technology of the time was insufficient for the wounds they had sustained.

ghost story

Ghostly things have been happening in and around the Lotz House since the Battle of Franklin. Since so many people died such painful and sudden deaths here, it is no wonder that spirits continue to haunt the area. Inside the house, things will often move around inexplicably. Small objects that have been set upon tables within the house will slide across the tables as terrified onlookers watch in disbelief. Coffee mugs, glasses, and vases are just some of the objects that have moved across tables by themselves.

Sometimes people within the house will hear the sound of battle drums beating outside. When they look outside, expecting to see some sort of reenactment going on, the streets are empty and the sound of drumming stop.

The interior of the house is not the only area that is haunted, however. In the front yard, people will often hear the sounds of battle. Gunshots, screams, and sobs will all echo through the empty night here. While historians will tell you that the Battle of Franklin lasted for a single night, those who visit the Lotz House know that the battle still rages.

visiting

While all throughout the year ghostly things will happen in and around the Lotz House, the paranormal activity reaches its peak on November 29, the anniversary of the battle. Since this was one of the few night battles during the war, a lot of the ghostly activity will actually happen after dark. The benefit of this is that the house is right along the street and you can easily walk in front of the house at night on November 29 or any night during the rest of the year. Bring your audio recorders and perhaps you'll catch some sounds of battle.

Another positive thing about visiting this area to search for ghosts is that there is actually a ghost tour that moves from the Lotz House to the Carter House. These tours, operated by Franklin on Foot (www.franklinonfoot.com), will tell you the ghost stories and explain exactly where to look for ghosts.

OAKLANDS HISTORIC HOUSE MUSEUM

900 N. Maney Ave., Murfreesboro, TN 37130

directions

Get on I-24 East and follow it for about 27 miles to Exit 78B, Old Fort Parkway, toward Murfreesboro. Follow Old Fort Parkway for a little more than 2 miles, where you'll need to veer left to stay on Old Fort Parkway. Stay on Old Fort Parkway for almost another mile, and then turn right onto West Loki Avenue. Follow this road for almost a half mile, and then turn right onto North Academy Street. Take the second left onto Evergreen Street. Take the second left onto North Maney Avenue. The street will dead-end into the museum.

history

The original structure for this historic mansion was built in 1813. At the time, it was a small, two-room brick structure that would eventually grow to the large, beautiful mansion that it is today. The families that owned the mansion during its early life were quite rich, and the mansion would become the social center of Murfreesboro, where some of the most important people of the time were entertained. Jefferson Davis visited the mansion during the Civil War. President Polk's wife visited the home at least once.

When the Civil War raged in central Tennessee, a small group of Union soldiers were camped on the grounds of the mansion. Confederate General Forrest attacked them to build his own foothold in Murfreesboro. A small battle broke out on the front lawn of the mansion, as the children in the house watched from an upstairs window.

After the war, the plantation began to fail because the entirety of its labor force had been slaves. Desperate to save the house, the Maney family sued the federal government for damages done to the house and grounds during the small battle that occurred on their lawn. The government dismissed the lawsuit.

The Maneys were able to retain ownership of the home until 1889, when they were forced to sell it to pay off debts. The house changed hands several more times until 1954, when it simply sat abandoned. For three years, vandals and thieves constantly broke into the abandoned house and stole and destroyed things. Finally, in 1958, the city purchased the property and eventually restored it.

ghost story

From the time that the house was restored to its original magnificence at the end of the 1950s, ghost stories began to circulate about the building and grounds. People will experience feelings of discomfort when within the house, especially when they are there by themselves. They will have no explanation for these feelings beyond having a vague sense that they are being watched.

Sometimes people inside the house will hear strange footsteps or even the sounds of breathing close by. When these sounds are investigated, the source is never found. People will see shadowy figures walking through the grounds at night. The figures quickly disappear whenever they are approached.

It seems that some of the employees have gotten used to the ghosts here. When we first asked about ghosts at Oaklands, one employee said that there were no ghosts. She said that sometimes they will hear footsteps or breathing sounds or see figures on the grounds but that there weren't really any ghost stories. Perhaps it's a testament to the frequency of the ghostly happenings here that things like this seem normal to those who are present most often.

visiting

Hours of operation are Tuesday through Saturday, 10 a.m. to 4 p.m. and Sunday, 1 p.m. to 4 p.m. The last tour each day begins one hour before closing. Admission to the house itself is $10, but the grounds are open to the public at no charge during daylight hours. To experience many of these ghosts, you have to actually enter the house itself, and this needs to be done during regular business hours. Some of the ghostly activity takes place outside on the grounds, though. This activity can be experienced even after the house and museum have closed for the night. Just make sure that you do not enter the property after dark, because it is posted that the grounds close at dusk.

RATTLE AND SNAP PLANTATION

1522 N. Main St., Mount Pleasant, TN 38474

directions

Take I-65 South for about 30 miles to Exit 53, the Saturn Parkway/TN 396 West exit. Follow this road for about 4.5 miles and then merge onto US 31 South. Follow this road for about 9 miles. Turn right onto US 43 South and follow this road for another 9.5 miles to the Zion Road ramp. At the end of the ramp, turn left onto Zion Road. Go for about a half mile, and then turn right onto Main Street. The Rattle and Snap Plantation house will be on your left.

history

While the name of this plantation may seem strange at first, this moniker has its origin in the way that the land was attained by its original owner, William Polk. Polk was a North Carolinian who was involved in a game of chance called "rattle and snap" with the governor of North Carolina. The game resulted in the governor losing 5,648 acres in Tennessee to William Polk, and Polk named the property Rattle and Snap because of this. Polk's four sons built houses on the large tract of land. In 1842, one of his sons, George Polk, built the Rattle and Snap Plantation house that still stands today. George is the only one of the sons who kept the original name of Rattle and Snap for his house.

The house stayed with the family for many years after George Polk passed away. By the middle of the 20th century, the house was abandoned by its owners and used as a barn. The house was used to store tobacco and other items that were grown on the land.

ghost story

Sallie Polk, George Polk's wife, is considered by many to be the ghost that haunts the Rattle and Snap Plantation house. Most of the ghostly activity that occurs in the house is limited to a single room in the mansion. The room was used by Sallie and George as the master bedroom when they inhabited the home in the mid-1800s.

What happens most frequently in the master bedroom is that the bed will often mess itself up. The bed will be nicely made, but even though no one enters the room in the interim, the sheets will be found crumpled and pushed aside the next time someone enters.

The lights in the master bedroom will turn on and off by themselves from time to time. Sometimes the lights will turn on or off while people are actually inside the room. Occasionally the lights will turn on during the night even though no one is in the building.

People will also smell roses and tobacco smoke when they enter the master bedroom, although no one can smoke in the room and there are no roses here. Yet these smells may have an explanation. The fact that the home stored tobacco when it was used as a barn could explain the tobacco odor. The rose smell could be subliminal because the room's wallpaper is decorated with roses.

visiting

Hauntings at large plantation houses can often be experienced both inside and outside and do not require you to enter to encounter them. Rattle and Snap is an exception to this. You need to actually enter the house on a tour in order to see this ghost, since the ghost is confined to the one bedroom. Without a reservation, you cannot even approach the house. There is a gate on the driveway that advertises trained attack dogs which will attack any trespassers.

Tours are $20 per person and require a reservation. This is the only way to see the haunted bedroom and experience the ghost here.

RIPPAVILLA PLANTATION

5700 Main St., Spring Hill, TN 37174

directions

Take I-65 South for about 30 miles to Exit 53, Saturn Parkway. Take the exit west toward Columbia/Spring Hill, and follow the road for about 4.5 miles. Take the exit for US 31 South/Main Street toward Columbia. Follow the road for a little more than a mile. The plantation will be on your left.

history

Years before the iconic plantation house itself was built, a man named Nathaniel Cheairs was born on this property in 1818 and grew up here. Eventually, he met a girl named Susan from nearby Spring Hill and asked his father for his blessing to marry her. Nathaniel's father disapproved of the marriage. Every male in the family for the previous four generations had married a girl named Sarah, and he would not have his son marrying a Susan. When Susan's father offered bricks from his factory to build them a nice home, Nathaniel's father relented, and Nathaniel and Susan were wed.

Nathaniel wanted the house to be perfect and to stand for more than 100 years. Several times during its construction he ordered the entire building torn down because he was concerned that it wasn't strong enough. The house was finally completed in the 1850s, giving the Cheairs family a few years to live there in peace before the Civil War.

When the Civil War broke out, the house became the headquarters for the Confederate Army of Tennessee. The house would actually change hands during the war, being at one time the headquarters for the Union army under Bull Nelson.

The darkest piece of history that the building sustained, though, was in 1862. That year, there was an outbreak of smallpox in the area, and Rippavilla served as a hospital for those affected by the disease. Many died painful deaths within the house.

ghost story

This plantation is considered one of the most paranormally active locations in all of Tennessee. There is no lack of ghostly activity between these walls, and those people who have conducted paranormal investigations here rarely come away disappointed.

One of the most active places in the house is Jenny's Room on the second floor. Within this room, people will feel uncomfortable and will hear what sounds like a child's voice. Investigators with audio recorders have recorded the ghostly voice of an older man within this room.

Nathaniel and Susan are seen throughout the house as well. Docents who have worked in the house see them walking around and recognize them clearly as the previous owners of the building. These two apparitions aren't the only two that are seen in the house. A small child is often seen playing on the front porch of the building. When the witnesses look away, the child vanishes and there are no children found on the property. Civil War soldiers are also seen throughout the house and the surrounding grounds.

As if these apparitions and voices aren't enough, witnesses will often see balls of light that float throughout the house. The color of the lights change from day to day. Sometimes they are blue, sometimes white or gold.

visiting

Finding the ghosts here involves entering the building while it is open to the public. It is open for business Monday through Saturday, 9:30 a.m. to 4:30 p.m., and Sunday, 1 p.m. to 4:30 p.m. The last tour each day starts at 3:30 p.m., and the tours cost $10 per person.

The plantation house has allowed paranormal groups from the area to investigate overnight on occasion. If you are part of a reputable, established paranormal investigation group, it couldn't hurt to contact the management of the property and ask if you can investigate there.

ROY ACUFF HOUSE

2800 block of Opryland Dr., Nashville, TN 37214

directions

From the heart of downtown, take Seventh Avenue North until you get to Charlotte Avenue. Turn left onto Charlotte Avenue and it will soon become James Robertson Parkway. Take the ramp onto US 31 E North/Ellington Parkway and follow this road for about 5 miles until the TN 155 East/Briley Parkway exit. Follow TN 155 East toward Opryland until you reach Exit 12, McGavock Pike West. Merge onto Music Valley Drive. You will take your first right and then your first left to bring you to the Opryland Plaza area. The Roy Acuff House is in the Opryland Plaza area near the Grand Ole Opry. It houses offices and a small museum.

history

Singer Roy Acuff was an important performer in the early history of country music and the Grand Ole Opry. Starting his music career in the early 1930s, Roy Acuff and his band, the Smokey Mountain Boys, are considered by many to be the reason that country music is so popular today. While country music started as having a more "bluegrass" and "hoedown" sound, Roy Acuff and his band moved the genre into the singer-based format that it has now become.

In 1938, Acuff was invited to join the Grand Ole Opry radio show, and he considered this one of the high points of his career. He stayed very active with the Grand Ole Opry until his death in 1992, going so far as building a home on the Opry Plaza adjacent to the Grand Ole Opry Theater so that he could be close to the action. Soon after his death in 1992 his home was made into a museum.

In 2010, a major flood hit Nashville and the Opry Plaza, damaging the house and many of the surrounding buildings. The building was one of the structures that was saved in the aftermath of the flood and is again open as a small museum.

ghost story

The Opry Plaza as a whole is filled with ghosts, but the ghostly activity at the Roy Acuff House didn't start until after his death in 1992. This leads many witnesses to believe that the ghost who is haunting this house is none other than Roy Acuff himself.

Lights throughout the building will turn on for several minutes and then turn off, even when the building is completely empty. People inside will hear footsteps throughout the building but when they search for the source of the sounds, they find no one. Objects in the house will sometimes mysteriously disappear and move to other locations throughout the building. An employee will be certain that he or she left something in a specific place but will find it several days later in a completely different room of the house.

Objects will also be seen moving by themselves within the house. Small objects on tables and mantels will slide across or sometimes fall to the floor. Chairs will move by themselves as well.

visiting

The Roy Acuff House is again open as a museum since being cleaned up after the flood. In order to hear the footsteps and perhaps witness objects moving inside the house, you would have to visit the small museum during daytime business hours, which are irregular, thus requiring an advance call. Since the house is right on the Opry Plaza, you can watch it at night to see if the lights turn on and off by themselves.

SAM DAVIS HOME
1399 Sam Davis Rd., Smyrna, TN 37167

directions
Exit downtown by taking I-24 East for about 19 miles to Exit 66B, Sam Ridley Parkway West. Follow Sam Ridley Parkway for a little more than 5 miles until the road forks at Jefferson Drive. Angle right at the fork to continue on Nissan Drive, and then take your first right onto Sam Davis Road. The Sam Davis Home will be on your right a little less than a half mile down the road.

history
Until he joined the Confederate army in 1861, not much is known about Sam Davis. We do know that he was a young Confederate soldier during the Civil War who was wounded at both the Battle of Shiloh and the Battle of Perryville. While his wounds at Shiloh allowed him to continue the fight, his wounds at Perryville prevented him from joining active combat. In order to still help the cause, Davis became a courier for the Confederacy.

On November 20, 1863, Davis was captured in Minor Hill, Tennessee, wearing a Confederate uniform and carrying important Union battle plans. Since he would not reveal the name of the source who provided him with the plans, he was considered ineligible as a prisoner of war and was sentenced to be hung. He stood steadfast in his conviction to keep the name of his informant secret. "I would rather die a thousand deaths than betray a friend," he said.

On his 21st birthday, November 27, Davis was marched to the gallows. Sickened by his young age, many Union soldiers in attendance pleaded with him to divulge the name of his informant, but Davis still refused. The officer in charge of pulling the lever to hang Davis was hesitant to go through with it. Davis's last words were, "Officer, I did my duty. Now you do yours."

Davis's father claimed the body, and Sam Davis was buried in the family plot at their home in Smyrna.

ghost story

The sound of weeping can often be heard within the house. Witnesses will hear it clearly coming from the next room, and then the sound will stop as soon as they turn the corner. Reportedly, Sam's mother, in the days following his death, would take out his old school uniform and weep over it for hours. Perhaps these crying sounds have made a permanent imprint upon the home.

The lights inside the building will sometimes act up at night. Employees who are sure that the building is closed and the lights are all off will notice that every light in the house is on as they approach the main road. As they drive back toward the house to extinguish the lights, the lights turn off by themselves.

Many apparitions are also seen in and around the house. Most of the apparitions on the property are seen in the rooms on the second floor, and they are most often observed by children. These witnesses will see white men in period dress and sometimes African American men and women in period dress in the rooms on the second floor.

Another apparition is often seen walking through the cemetery on the property as well. Witnesses who encounter this apparition report that he looks exactly like Oscar Davis, Sam's brother.

visiting

When visiting this house, keep in mind that the house and grounds are open for tours every month of the year except January. They are open from 9 a.m. to 5 p.m. during the summer months, and 10 a.m. to 4 p.m. for the remainder of the year. Admission is $8.50. There are also ghost tours of the house on weekends in October. You almost need to visit during regular business hours in order to experience the ghosts here since the grounds are closed to the public outside of these hours. Beyond this, the best time to find a ghost here is during the month of December. Activity is most frequent during this month, as it was when Sam Davis's body was laid in the house while his burial plot was prepared.

SMITH-TRAHERN MANSION
101 McClure St., Clarksville, TN 37040

directions

Overlooking the Cumberland River, this large mansion sits near Resthaven Memorial Gardens and Austin Peay State University in Clarksville. Take I-65 North to I-24 West. Follow I-24 West for 34 miles until you get to Exit 11 toward Clarksville. Follow TN 76 West off the exit for a little more than 11 miles until you come to McClure Street. Turn right onto McClure Street. The house will be on the hillside above the river.

history

This building was built in 1859, shortly before the Civil War, and was home to one of the area's most prominent tobacco exporters, a man named Christopher Smith. As a businessman in the tobacco industry, Smith made a lot of money and was able to afford the luxurious mansion that overlooks the Cumberland River.

One day Smith took a riverboat trip down the Cumberland River and the Mississippi River all the way to New Orleans to discuss business with some possible investors. While in New Orleans, Smith contracted yellow fever and died of the disease.

News eventually reached Christopher Smith's wife about his untimely death, and she was completely devastated to the point of psychosis. She refused to believe that he had died and would sit by the upstairs window overlooking the Cumberland, waiting for either her husband or the body of her husband to return. Her husband's body was put on a ship and sent up the Mississippi River toward home in Clarksville but met with calamity along the way. Something on board ignited, and the riverboat exploded. All on board, including the body of Christopher Smith, were lost. His wife vigilantly kept watch at the upstairs window for many years until she eventually passed away from old age.

ghost story

Death has a way of stopping some people from accomplishing life goals. In the case of Christopher Smith's wife, who was determined to watch for her husband until he returned, her own death seems to have done little to dissuade her from her mission. Many people who approach the mansion today, be it during the day or at night, will report seeing a woman staring out of the upstairs window toward the river. When the mysterious face in the window is investigated, there is no one there. Many claim that this is the ghost of Christopher Smith's wife, still staring out at the river waiting for her husband, unaware that he will never return.

Her face in the window may be the most often experienced ghost here, but employees and visitors to the house have reported strange things inside as well. Many people will describe general feelings of discomfort. They will feel as if they are being watched by some unseen presence and will sometimes hear phantom footsteps following them throughout the house.

visiting

Visiting this haunted location does not necessarily entail going when the building is open to the public. Since many of the sightings of this ghost occur from the exterior of the building, looking up to the second-floor window, this ghost can be encountered even when the building itself is closed. If you are there after dark, though, be careful not to trespass. A road that approaches the house on the left side is actually a driveway into a cemetery that closes at dark. The road that faces the front of the building is rather far from the front and would make seeing a face in the upstairs window impossible after dark. The grounds are closed at night, and nearby residents would almost certainly report anyone trespassing on the grounds of so historic a landmark.

This being said, it is probably better to simply visit this ghost during the day. For a very small admission (only $2 for adults), you can actually enter the house and attempt to experience the ghosts inside for yourself. Even if you are unwilling to pay the $2 admission, daylight offers a much clearer view of the upstairs window and the grounds are open to the public, so you can get a much closer view of the window than is possible at night.

SUNNYSIDE MANSION

3000 Granny White Pike, Nashville, TN 37204

directions

Easily reached from downtown Nashville, Sunnyside Mansion is only about 2 miles from the very heart of the city. Simply take 12th Avenue South. After about 2 miles, 12th Avenue changes its name to Granny White Pike. Near that point, you'll find Sunnyside Mansion on the left. It is actually in Sevier Park.

history

From the time the mansion was built in the 1850s to the beginning of the Civil War, nothing tragic occurred within this building. During the Civil War, more specifically during the Battle of Nashville, the mansion sat between Confederate and Union forces. As the number of wounded in the area began to increase, local buildings, including Sunnyside, were turned into makeshift hospitals. Wounded men from both sides of the battle would pile into Sunnyside Mansion for medical treatment. Unfortunately, the medical care of the time was limited, and many died within the building's walls.

Strangely, though, the number of people who died in the building during the Battle of Nashville in the 1860s is far less than the number who died there after the turn of the century. In the early 1900s, the building was used as a tuberculosis sanitarium. At that time, there was no cure for this disease of the lungs, and it was highly contagious. In order to get the infected away from the populous, sanitariums were set up across the country. Sunnyside Mansion served as one of these sanitariums, and many of the infected who were housed here died.

ghost story

Experiences with the ghosts here at Sunnyside have been mostly auditory. People will hear moans and screams most often, both inside and outside the building. Witnesses to the hauntings will also often hear the sounds of coughing. When they investigate these coughs, no one is there.

These strange sounds are not the only ghosts here. People will also see full-bodied apparitions throughout the house and the surrounding park. Sometimes these figures are seen as dark shadows that suddenly disappear. Other times, these figures appear lying on the ground and are accompanied by the ghostly moans and screams.

visiting

The building itself is not accessible. Tourists and ghosthunters are unable to enter the house for any reason at any time. This doesn't mean that you cannot see the ghosts here, however. Many of the ghostly occurrences happen in the area immediately surrounding the house. This area is all parkland and is easily accessible and free to anyone who may want to visit.

A strong word of caution, though: This building is not in the safest area of town. It would be in your best interest not to visit this area after dark. To do so could be dangerous and not worth the risk.

TRAVELLERS REST PLANTATION

636 Farrell Pkwy., Nashville, TN 37220

directions

Take I-65 South to Exit 78B, TN 255 West/Harding Place. At the end of the exit ramp, make a slight right onto Harding Place. About a half mile down the road, turn left onto Franklin Road, and then follow it for about a mile. Turn left onto Farrell Road, and then take your second right onto Farrell Parkway. The entrance to the plantation will be on your left, just past the railroad tracks and across from the park.

history

Nearly eight miles from the city's center, this plantation was actually quite isolated from the bulk of Nashville's population. In 1799, when building the house, Judge John Overton named his new home Golgotha, a biblical name meaning "the place of the skull." While the cellar was dug out for the house, they unearthed human skulls and discovered that the area had been a Native American burial ground which stretched out for acres all across the plantation's land and the surrounding hills. The burial ground had sat undisturbed for about 600 years.

Judge Overton was a circuit judge from the area who would often travel for weeks on end. It was this constant travel that eventually encouraged the judge to change the name of his plantation house to Travellers Rest.

While the home was an important part of the Overton family for the next 150 years, nothing really tragic ever occurred at the house. Yet the house would grow over the years in rather strange ways. New wings would be added, and adjacent buildings would be assimilated into the home. At one point, there were four rooms in the upstairs of the house, none of which could be accessed from another without first descending one of the home's four staircases and then ascending to another room.

ghost story

Often ghost stories will surface about the Travellers Rest Plantation home. Perhaps they are a result of the family who lived here for so many years or the constant renovations that were done to the building, or perhaps they date back to the Native American burial ground which once occupied the site.

Both visitors and docents have heard the sounds of voices. When these voices are investigated, no one is present. Others will hear children giggling in the children's room or hear footsteps or doors slamming throughout the building. Small objects in the home will move on their own, and people walking up the main stairwell have reported some unseen force pushing past them.

Several apparitions are seen throughout the building as well. A man in a top hat is sometimes observed in the house. A lady without legs is seen floating from the sitting room to the children's room on occasion. Despite her lack of legs, you can still hear her shoes walking across the floor. Another lady is glimpsed on the second-floor balcony looking out across the plantation. Confederate soldiers also appear across the grounds and on the balcony overlooking the plantation.

The building has a lot of trouble with its security system at night. Motion sensors throughout the house will go off even when the building has been locked up and is empty. Sometimes, the front or back door of the building will somehow open by itself in the middle of the night, setting off the alarms.

visiting

In order to access the plantation, you have to visit during regular business hours and pay the $10 admission. It is open from April through December, Monday through Saturday, 10 a.m. to 4 p.m., Sunday 1 p.m. to 4 p.m. (shorter hours in winter). Admission includes a guided tour of the home and the ability to roam the grounds.

TWO RIVERS MANSION

3130 McGavock Pike, Nashville, TN 37214

directions

From Downtown, take I-40 East for about 6 miles to Exit 215B, the Briley Parkway/
TN 155 North exit. Follow the parkway for about 2 miles to Exit 8; then take the
Lebanon Pike exit toward Donelson. Turn right onto Lebanon Pike and continue until
you reach McGavock Pike. Turn left on McGavock Pike and follow the road three
intersections past the railroad tracks to Two Rivers Parkway. The Two Rivers Mansion
will be past Two Rivers Parkway on your left.

history

The mansion itself was built by David McGavock in 1859 and acquired its name
because the 1,100 acres of land that the McGavocks occupied sat between the
Cumberland and the Stones rivers. Much of the original property was once used as a

burial ground for the Native Americans who occupied the area (see Two Rivers Golf Course chapter). Later, the land was used in the aftermath of several Civil War battles as a mass grave for many casualties there.

The mansion is one of the earliest examples of Italianate architecture in the country and is very well preserved. The mansion itself was owned by the McGavock family for three generations, from its genesis in 1859 until 1965. In 1965, the property was purchased by the City of Nashville and was listed on the National Register of Historic Places. Today, the mansion and grounds are used as a venue for weddings and can be rented out for other events.

ghost story

Very frequently, when the building is quiet and nearly empty, people will hear strange things throughout the mansion. Footsteps will echo through the halls. Doors will unlatch and creak. It will sound very much as if other people are inside the house even when they are not.

Visitors will also feel uncomfortable and even unwelcome inside the house. They will often feel as if they are being watched by some unseen presence. Sometimes these

ghosts are actually seen. Figures will be observed walking through the halls and rooms of the mansion. These figures vanish whenever they are approached.

Lights throughout the mansion will also turn on and off by themselves. This will happen sometimes after the building has been locked up for the evening. Even though the building is completely empty, witnesses will see lights flickering inside. Employees at the building also report that items they have left lying about throughout the mansion have mysteriously vanished, only to reappear at a later time in a different place.

visiting

Unfortunately the building itself is not open to the public for tours. The only way to gain access to the building is to rent it out for an event of some sort. If you are interested in renting the building for an event, you can make an appointment to receive a private tour of the house. If you're not going to rent the place but you still want to see some ghostly activity here, you can always watch the building and the grounds at night. People will sometimes encounter figures here and the lights in the mansion will occasionally flicker by themselves at night.

SECTION III

bars and restaurants

BATTLE GROUND BREWERY AND RESTAURANT

108 Bridge St., Franklin, TN 37064

directions

Right on the shore of the Harpeth River, to get here from Nashville simply take I-65 South from downtown for about 11 miles until you reach Exit 71 toward Brentwood. Turn right onto Concord Road (TN 253) and then, a little more than a half mile down the road, turn left onto Franklin Road. Follow Franklin Road for a little more than 6 miles until you reach First Avenue North. Turn right onto First Avenue, and then take the first left onto Bridge Street. The Battle Ground Brewery is the large brown building on your right.

history

On the night of November 30, 1864, death and destruction reigned just across the Harpeth River as the Battle of Franklin raged. Despite the fact that the battle was one of the bloodiest of the Civil War and it occurred so near to what is today the Battle Ground Brewery & Restaurant, the ghosts here are more likely a result of another slice of history from the area.

The building itself was built in 1905 as the county's first jail. Some of the worst offenders in the area resided here as they waited for their day in court. The county sheriff himself had living space in the building for himself and his family, separate from the prisoners who were kept in the back of the building.

Court was often held within the building for many of the prisoners. In the early part of the 1900s, many prisoners who were convicted were sent to the larger prisons throughout the state, but if the offense was severe enough, they were sometimes sentenced to hang. If a prisoner was sentenced to death between 1905 and 1915, they were hung inside the building near the site of the bar area today.

ghost story

Several strange things will happen with some regularity here at the Battle Ground Brewery & Restaurant. The ghostly phenomenon reported most often is the sound of strange, sourceless noises throughout the building. Sometimes these sounds are simply footsteps that seem to follow people around, but more often witnesses will hear what resembles a cell door slamming shut, perhaps some remnant of the jail cells that were once in the back of the building.

Another strange thing that will happen at the restaurant is that a certain object left somewhere will mysteriously disappear. Just when the object seems to have vanished forever, it will just as suddenly reappear in the same place that it had originally been left.

Shadowy figures are also seen throughout the building from time to time. Witnesses will glimpse a dark figure out of the corner of their eye, but when they go to investigate, they find no one there.

visiting

If you enter the building with the intention of finding some ghosts, those who work there are generally happy to tell you stories or show you around. Keep in mind, though, that this is still an operating restaurant, and during busier times the employees may not have time to talk about the ghosts.

The building can be entered only during regular business hours. It is open every day of the week from 11 a.m. until midnight. The meals are not expensive, so this would be a great haunted restaurant to stop in, have a meal, and maybe find a ghost.

BEER SELLAR

107 Church St., Nashville, TN 37201

directions

Near the heart of downtown Nashville, less than a block from the Cumberland River, the Beer Sellar's cavernous entrance descends from street level. From Broadway, simply take Second Avenue north until you reach Church Street. Turn right onto Church Street. The entrance to the Beer Sellar will be on your right just before the Riverfront Tavern.

history

Events from this building's history that may have caused the hauntings are somewhat hard to determine. The building itself has a lot of history, which exists from the earlier days of Nashville, back when Second Avenue was still called Market Street. The building was around during the Civil War as well, when many of the buildings in the area were used as temporary Civil War hospitals.

Throughout its more recent history, the building sits just at the very edge of the Nashville nightclub district and yet has managed to be more a venue for the locals than it has ever been for the tourists.

ghost story

Frequently, people who walk inside the Beer Sellar will experience strange feelings. They will sense that they are being watched even though they cannot see anyone watching them. They will feel chills crawl down their spine or experience general feelings of discomfort or dread. These feelings will often be overpowering, but the people experiencing them will never be able to find any concrete reason behind them.

People also hear noises quite often within this building. Some will hear footsteps although there is no one there; others will hear phantom voices or bangs and knocks that have no earthly explanation.

Perhaps the creepiest thing that happens here at the Beer Sellar is that objects will move around the building by themselves. An employee or patron will leave something in one place and will leave for the night or go elsewhere within the building. When they return to the item that they had left, it has vanished. Only after a significant amount of searching do they find that the item has simply moved to a different place within

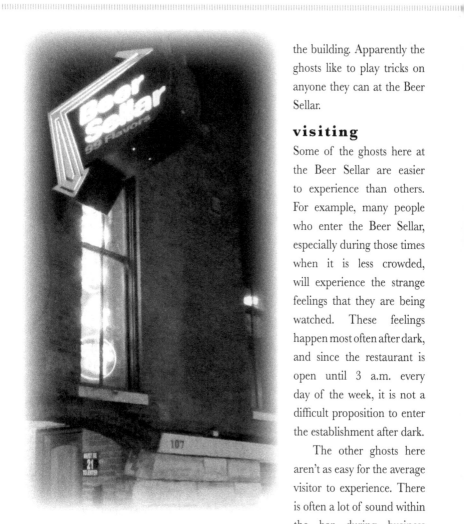

the building. Apparently the ghosts like to play tricks on anyone they can at the Beer Sellar.

visiting

Some of the ghosts here at the Beer Sellar are easier to experience than others. For example, many people who enter the Beer Sellar, especially during those times when it is less crowded, will experience the strange feelings that they are being watched. These feelings happen most often after dark, and since the restaurant is open until 3 a.m. every day of the week, it is not a difficult proposition to enter the establishment after dark.

The other ghosts here aren't as easy for the average visitor to experience. There is often a lot of sound within the bar during business hours, so it is hard to differentiate between ghostly noises and actual people. Also, for customers, objects rarely move on their own, and even if they were to, it would be difficult to tell if a person moved the object or if it actually moved by itself. These ghosts are most often experienced by employees or others who are in the building alone before it opens or after it closes.

BUFFALO BILLIARDS

154 Second Ave. N., Nashville, TN 37201

directions

Buffalo Billiards is in the heart of downtown Nashville, near many of the other locations in this book that are on Broadway and Second Avenue. If you take Second Avenue north from Broadway, Buffalo Billiards will be on your right near the Coyote Ugly Bar and The Melting Pot restaurant.

history

The street that is today known as Second Avenue was known as Market Street in Nashville's early days and was completely populated with retail establishments selling all varieties of necessities to the Nashvillians of the time. Many of the buildings here, including the structure that houses Buffalo Billiards, are original from that time.

When the Civil War broke out in the area, injured from many of the local battles were brought to downtown Nashville and some of the buildings were used as hospital space. Although there is no evidence suggesting that the Buffalo Billiards building was used in this way, it is certainly possible since much of the store space down Market Street and up Broadway became medical facilities.

More recently, Second Avenue and Broadway have become a tourist trap, filled with bars and honky-tonks. Buffalo Billiards is another one of these bars along Second Avenue in the center of current Nashville culture.

ghost story

Like many ghosts, the ghosts here at Buffalo Billiards act up when there are not many people inside the building. Most often the activity happens just after the place opens or just before it closes.

Often, the hauntings take the form of strange sounds. People will hear billiard balls hitting one another even when no one is playing pool. People will hear footsteps behind them and then turn around and find no one there. Glasses will clink together but those hearing them clink cannot see any glasses moving. All kinds of strange and inexplicable sounds will echo throughout the bar when it's quiet enough to notice them.

The other ghostly occurrence in Buffalo Billiards is that the lights will turn on and off by themselves. This happens most often when the employees are opening up for the day or closing down for the night.

visiting

Ghostly activity seems to happen most often here when it is quietest. This is typically just before closing time, which is between 1 and 3 a.m. depending on the day of the week, or just after opening, which is between 1 and 2 p.m. most days. This would be the best time to visit Buffalo Billiards if you are going there with the intention of looking for ghosts.

CAPTAIN D'S

2633 Lebanon Pike, Nashville, TN 37210

directions

You will leave downtown by taking I-40 East for about 6 miles to the Briley Parkway exit, Exit 215B. Follow this road for about 2 miles to the Lebanon Pike exit, Exit 8. Turn right onto Lebanon Pike, and follow the road for a little more than 4 miles. Captain D's will be on your left.

history

On February 16, 1997, Paul Dennis Reid entered this Captain D's restaurant before they opened, supposedly in order to apply for a job. Instead, Reid forced an employee and the manager into the back cooler of the restaurant and tied their hands and feet. Then, he executed both the employee and the manager by shooting them in cold blood. He ended up stealing whatever money he could get his hands on, which included large amounts of coins from the cash register. He used this money to place a down payment on a car.

Reid would go on to do the same thing at a McDonald's in Hermitage (see McDonald's chapter) and a Baskin-Robbins in Clarksville before getting caught. He is currently sitting on death row awaiting his own execution.

ghost story

Normally, people don't associate a place like Captain D's with ghosts, but a supernatural presence seems constantly at play here. Despite the dark history of the place, the spirit here seems quite benevolent.

People inside the restaurant, especially employees, report that they often experience feelings of a presence within the building. They say that they feel as if they are being observed despite the fact that no one is around them. Sometimes they will actually hear footsteps or other indicators that someone is there with them, but upon closer examination, they find no one.

Witnesses who describe these feelings of being observed report that the presence does not seem malevolent at all, but rather that it seems more to be watching over them than anything. Perhaps one of the victims of the killer has come back to protect those in the restaurant.

visiting

Entering this building in order to visit its protective ghost should be done during regular business hours. Since the feelings of a presence seem to happen exclusively inside, you would need to visit the restaurant when it is open. Most of the strange feelings here usually happen in the morning while the employees are opening the restaurant or soon after opening, perhaps since this was when the murders took place.

FLYING SAUCER

111 10th Ave. S., Nashville, TN 37203

directions

Very near the heart of Nashville's entertainment district, the Flying Saucer is actually inside the giant Union Station building. It is on 10th Avenue near Broadway. Since it is part of the old Union Station, it is immediately behind the giant Union Station Hotel.

history

The Flying Saucer was originally part of the Union Station train depot building and was used as a baggage claim area for many of the trains arriving at the station. Thousands of young men returning from war went through the emotion of meeting their loved ones here in this area. Beyond this, during the aftermath of the 1918 train wreck, the baggage claim area was used as a morgue for the victims of the catastrophe.

When the 1960s rolled around, most business to the Union Station had faded. Only a couple of trains came through the station by then. In 1979, the entire building was abandoned and it remained so for nearly 20 years. Today, this part of the building houses a bar called the Flying Saucer.

ghost story

If you were to ask any employee at the Flying Saucer what part of the bar is haunted, they would tell you without fail that it is the billiards room. Strange things happen in the billiards room, and actually quite often. Since this area was once the baggage claim for the haunted Union Station, people attribute the ghosts to this piece of history.

Things will often move on their own in the billiards room. The money slots in the pool tables will slide in and out when no one is there touching them. Pool cues will suddenly fall when they are resting against the walls. Chairs will slide across the floor. Drinks will fall down and sometimes simply slide off the tables. Not only do so many things move inexplicably here, this phenomenon seems to happen quite frequently. The billiards room has gained a reputation for this activity. Local news stations have even aired stories about the ghosts in the billiards room.

Another ghostly phenomenon that happens a lot in the billiards room involves the television sets situated around the room. The televisions will turn on and off by themselves. When the televisions are placed on mute, they will suddenly change channels to a station with nothing but static and the volume will come on full blast.

And if these ghostly stories aren't enough, apparitions are also seen in this room. The apparitions aren't usually walking around the billiards room with the other patrons but are actually only viewed in the room's mirrors. An unsuspecting patron will oftentimes glance into the mirror and see someone standing behind them who isn't actually present in the room.

visiting

The employees at the Flying Saucer fully embrace their ghosts and have even invited ghost investigation groups into the bar in order to try to capture evidence of these phenomena. If you're not a part of a paranormal group, though, your best bet for experiencing these ghosts is to simply go to the bar when it's open and wait in the pool room. The bar opens at 11 a.m. or noon every day and remains open until 1 a.m. during the week and 2 a.m. on the weekends. Make sure you glance into the mirrors every once in a while, as you never know who's watching.

GRECIANS GREEK AND ITALIAN

122 W. Franklin St., Gallatin, TN 37066

directions

Head north on I-65 to Exit 95, TN 386 North. Take TN 386 North toward Hendersonville/Gallatin for 17 miles, and then angle right onto Red River Road. Less than a half mile down the road, turn left onto Broadway then take your second right onto North Water Street. Take the third left onto Franklin Street. Grecians Greek and Italian will be on your left.

history

Existing at this site since the mid-1800s, this building was originally used as the Sumner County jail. Many of the area's worst criminals were housed here from the mid-1800s all the way into the 20th century. For many years, negative energy had time to build within this structure until the jail was moved across Water Street to Smith Street and the old jail was left empty.

The building was eventually taken over by a series of restaurants. The most famous one to grace the site was a Mexican restaurant named Loco Lupes. Eventually, Loco

Lupes was forced to declare bankruptcy, and the building was taken over by the new Oliver's Restaurant. Eventually Oliver's went out of business as well and Grecians moved in.

ghost story

Here in this building, there is a large variety of paranormal activity. There are two floors to the building, and the paranormal phenomena on each floor differ.

On the second floor of the building, people will hear the sound of doors slamming. Sometimes, the sound will resemble a normal wooden door, but other times, the sound is more like a cell door slamming shut and echoing throughout the building. When these sounds are heard upstairs, people downstairs don't hear them at all. Other witnesses upstairs will hear deep angry voices or violent knocking on the walls. People both upstairs and downstairs will detect footsteps walking up and down the stairs even when no one is present.

Downstairs, the activity seems to affect the plumbing more than anything else. Toilets will flush by themselves and water faucets will turn on and then turn off when no is one nearby.

visiting

To enter the building, you will have to visit during regular business hours and probably have a meal here. The prices are reasonable for the meals that they serve. For a dinner for two people with drinks, you would probably spend around $40. Lunch prices are a little cheaper, and the building is not as crowded at that time. The restaurant closes at 9 p.m. every day except Sunday when it closes at 2 p.m. Finding a time that is less busy, such as late on a weekday night or at lunch during the week, would be your best bet to experience the ghosts here.

HARD ROCK CAFE

100 Broadway, Nashville, TN 37201

directions

The Hard Rock Cafe is right in the heart of downtown Nashville, just a block away from the river. It is at the corner of Broadway and occupies the block between First and Second avenues. You can't miss it; just look for the giant neon guitar.

history

Resting underneath the glitzy exterior of this building lies a rather dark history. The building is on Broadway and Second Avenue, two of the city's main thoroughfares ever since its inception. In Nashville's early history, Second Avenue was filled with stores and merchants while Broadway held hotels, businesses, and entertainment venues.

The building where the Hard Rock Cafe is currently located was the city's first brothel. Men from all stations of life would often end up here to satisfy their more carnal desires. Many of the women who worked here, especially in the dark days following the Civil War, had little other choice than to sell their bodies for money. Many of these women came from a higher class before the war. The war made them destitute, however, and forced them into prostitution in order to eat and feed their families.

After the building's years as a brothel, it eventually became a bar and restaurant. In 1994, the Hard Rock Cafe opened here and is still in operation to this day.

ghost story

Needless to say, the Hard Rock plays host to several ghosts. Since the ghosts are never seen, it is hard to pinpoint the exact moment in history when they originated. The ghosts do tend to make their presence known from time to time at the restaurant.

One favorite pastime of these ghosts is stacking chairs. After everyone has left for the evening, chairs will stack themselves throughout the restaurant. When the employees return in the morning to open for the day, they will find several chairs stacked very differently than they were the night before.

The chairs aren't the only objects that move in this building. Glasses will slide off of bars and tables by themselves. Pictures and exhibits will shift. Liquor bottles will fall off the shelf. All kinds of smaller objects will move while everyone watching can see that there is no earthly reason that they should be moving.

Also, ghosts tend to tap unsuspecting patrons on the shoulder. Visitors will feel a tap on their shoulder and will turn around only to find that no one is there.

visiting

You would need to visit the Hard Rock Cafe during normal business hours in order to experience its ghosts. The restaurant is open Sunday through Thursday, 11 a.m. to 10 p.m.; Friday and Saturday, 11 a.m. to midnight (shop hours are reduced). The building tends to get really busy on weekend nights, so you may want to opt for a different time to visit the Hard Rock. Ghostly activity seems to occur at any time of the day or night, so it doesn't really matter what time you show up.

McDONALD'S

3470 Lebanon Rd., Hermitage, TN 37076

directions

Exit downtown by taking I-40 East to Old Hickory Boulevard, Exit 221A. Take the exit toward The Hermitage. Follow this road for about 3 miles before turning left onto Lebanon Road. The McDonald's will be on your right at the intersection with Bonnabrook Drive.

history

On March 23, 1997, two workers at the McDonald's on Lebanon Road were taking garbage to the dumpster behind the restaurant when a man approached them with a gun. He forced the workers to let him into the building so that he could rob them. He led the four people working in the building to the storeroom, suggesting that he would lock them there while he made his escape. Things turned quite a bit tragic there as the robber executed three of the workers before running out of bullets. He stabbed the final worker 17 times before fleeing the scene.

The fourth worker survived, eventually identifying the killer. He had done the same thing at a local Captain D's restaurant (see Captain D's chapter) and a Baskin-Robbins. All told, the killer had executed seven people. Fast food restaurants in the Nashville area began closing earlier, and many began requiring employees to have stickers on their cars so that local law enforcement could tell if any cars in the parking lots didn't belong there.

ghost story
Nothing seems to be able to erase the memory of what happened that terrible night. The paranormal activity reported most often at this McDonald's is a simple feeling of unease. People who are in the dining room report feeling unwelcome and sometimes sensing they are being watched. People will often feel chills crawling down their spine while inside the restaurant or when behind the restaurant near the dumpster.

Apparitions are also frequently reported at this McDonald's. Out of the corner of an eye, witnesses will glimpse someone walking into the building. When they look toward the figure, the figure has completely vanished.

visiting
Never closing, the drive-through window at this McDonald's is open 24 hours a day. The dining room is only open until 11 p.m. though. The windows to the restaurant are easily visible, so if any shadowy figures are walking around inside, you can see them at any time of the night. If you want to enter the building and experience the discomfort of being near the ghosts inside, you'll have to visit before 11 p.m.

McFADDEN'S RESTAURANT AND SALOON

134 Second Ave. N., Nashville, TN 37201

directions

In the heart of downtown Nashville on Second Avenue just north of Broadway, you'll find McFadden's. If you're going down Second from Broadway, McFadden's will be on your right, adorned with flags.

history

Second Avenue holds an important place in the history of Nashville. From the city's founding in 1779, Second Avenue has been a prominent business district. Hardware, groceries, and mercantile goods were all sold along this strip, originally called Market Street. Many of the buildings, including the one that currently houses McFadden's Restaurant and Saloon, are well over 100 years old and countless people have walked through these doors and made their livings here.

In the building's recent history, it was a bar called the Market Street Brewery and Pub House, but this business was replaced by McFadden's Restaurant and Saloon, a chain restaurant that began in New York City.

ghost story

The hauntings here at McFadden's often involve objects moving for no apparent reason. Throughout the entire restaurant, things will move around, and those who witness the strange phenomena will have absolutely no idea what is happening.

Furniture moves most often here. Chairs and tables will slide across the floor even when no one is anywhere near them. Drinking glasses will also move inexplicably. The glasses will sometimes slide off the tables and shatter on the floor. The glasses will at times slowly creep across the bar as patrons and employees alike watch in wonder.

The light fixtures in this building will also move with no apparent cause. Several hanging light fixtures situated throughout the restaurant will occasionally start to sway for no reason. There is no breeze to move them and no person on the floor above to cause the swaying.

visiting

Entering McFadden's is possible seven days a week from 11 a.m. to 3 a.m. The prices are reasonable, and it is a popular place to go in downtown Nashville on Friday and Saturday nights. The only way to enter the building to watch for the resident ghosts is to go inside during business hours. You are more likely to experience objects moving inexplicably if you visit the building during hours when it is less busy. This means it is probably best to go around 3 p.m. after the lunch rush has ended but before the dinner rush begins, or late at night during the week when most patrons have left for the night.

McNAMARA'S IRISH PUB

2740 Old Lebanon Rd., Nashville, TN 37214

directions

Reaching McNamara's Irish Pub involves taking I-40 East for 6 miles to Exit 215B, the Briley Parkway exit. Follow this road for 2 miles to Exit 8, Lebanon Pike. Take a right onto Lebanon Pike off of the exit, toward Donelson. Continue for about a mile and a half, and then turn left onto Old Lebanon Road. The pub will be on the right.

history

No one would guess that this buiding is a pub when looking at it from the outside. It actually resembles an old plantation house more than the Irish pub that it actually is. This has something to do with the building's original purpose. Before becoming McNamara's, this was a restaurant called the Plantation House. But predating even the Plantation House restaurant, this building actually housed a funeral parlor. Bodies were constantly moving in and out of the building, and mourning relatives would often hold wakes here. Much death and mourning have left a mark upon this building. In the basement, the funeral home had a crematorium that was used to cremate many of the bodies that came here.

ghost story

Some people who enter McNamara's say that inexplicable feelings of sadness overcome them. The people who experience this will be incredibly happy and carefree one minute but will suddenly be struck with feelings of sadness and depression.

Sometimes, when the building is mostly empty and quiet, people will hear the sounds of sobbing coming from all around them. There is no one here crying, but the sounds are clearly present nonetheless. Perhaps these sobs are remnants of the mourning that dominated this building in its early life.

Certain people will glimpse shadow figures roaming throughout the building. These witnesses will see a dark shadowy figure out of the corner of an eye and will turn toward the figure only to find that it has vanished. These shadow figures are observed most often by employees visiting the basement of the building.

visiting

This Irish pub does live up to its name. The pub is often frequented by Irishmen, and it features live Irish music Thursday through Sunday. The pub is open until 10 p.m. Tuesday–Thursday and Sunday, and until 1 a.m. Friday and Saturday. The pub is closed on Monday. Enter the building anytime during normal business hours if you want to see or experience the ghosts here. Unfortunately, the basement is closed to the public, so you'll have to look for ghosts on the main floor of the building.

THE MELTING POT

166 Second Ave. N., Nashville, TN 37201

directions

The Melting Pot is in the heart of downtown Nashville on Second Avenue North. It will be on the right side of the street if you're going down Second Avenue from Broadway, and it is adjacent to the Buffalo Billiards and Coyote Ugly bars.

history

Enamored with one another, two employees at The Melting Pot wanted nothing more than to spend the rest of their lives together. However, they were young, and their parents did not approve of the relationship. They were forbidden to see each other.

Despite this hardship, the two continued to see each other secretly, and they remained relatively happy, devising a plan to save some money and eventually run away together. This was all brought to an abrupt end when the girl's mother caught the two of them together. The young girl's parents then forced her to quit her job so that they wouldn't have to worry about the couple secretly meeting anymore.

Crushed, the girl sneaked away one night and met her lover at The Melting Pot, where they decided that they would be together forever no matter what. They went to the restaurant's basement and killed themselves. When their bodies were found, their hands were touching.

ghost story

Even though the only people permitted to enter the downstairs of the building are employees, most of the hauntings at The Melting Pot occur in the basement. The two lovers are often encountered downstairs but oftentimes seem more frightened of the living than the living are of them. The young man is frequently seen peeking around storage boxes in the basement. No one is found when the witness goes to investigate. The young woman is often observed crying uncontrollably. The lights in the basement will also flicker inexplicably, a phenomenon that employees usually attribute to the doomed couple.

Ghostly activity also happens throughout the remainder of the restaurant, although not as often. In the women's restroom, stall doors will open and close and the water will turn on by itself. Drinking glasses sometimes slide across tables for no reason. It seems that the star-crossed lovers have managed to remain together despite the wishes of their parents.

visiting

Unfortunately, the basement is used for storage and as an employee area, so it is off-limits to the public. That's OK, though, because the hauntings have been known to extend into the restaurant area itself. If you are in the mood for a nice romantic dinner, make a reservation at The Melting Pot and perhaps encounter a ghost who is there for romance as well.

MERCHANTS RESTAURANT

401 Broadway, Nashville, TN 37203

directions

This restaurant is located on Broadway in the center of downtown Nashville at the corner of Fourth Avenue.

history

Two pieces of history have possibly influenced the spiritual behavior here at the restaurant. First, since this building was an important hotel in the early 20th century, it is possible that parts of it were used as a brothel. Unfortunately, records of such places were not kept at that time, and we were unable to find any concrete evidence of this.

The other historical report that more likely inspires the ghosts here is more easily verifiable and did actually happen. This building was built in 1892 as the Merchant's Hotel. The bottom floor was inhabited by a pharmacy, and the third floor functioned as a wholesale drug company. At one point during the pharmacy's existence, the pharmacist's son suffered from depression. He hung himself on the third floor of the building in front of a window that overlooked Broadway.

ghost story

Due to the suicide that happened here, the third floor of this building is home to most of the ghostly activity. Employees who have gone up alone to this floor report footsteps following them, strange figures that disappear into nothingness, and a general sense of discomfort.

Employees aren't the only ones who experience strange phenomena at the Merchants Restaurant, though. Oftentimes, customers will approach the front door of the building with the intention of entering and will for some reason glance up to one of the windows on the third floor. They will report seeing the silhouette of a man hanging by his neck and swinging back and forth in front of the window. Sometimes the customers will dismiss it as a trick of the light until someone else mentions it. Other times, the customers will become so disturbed that they will report in a panic to the nearest employee that a man has just hung himself on the third floor. The employee will generally know better than to investigate.

visiting

Normally, you would need to enter the building during business hours, which are 11 a.m. until midnight Sunday–Wednesday, and 11 a.m. until 2 a.m. Thursday–Saturday. The third floor of the building is unfortunately not open to the public, so there is no way to access the floor unless you work for the restaurant.

This isn't to say that it is impossible to encounter the ghosts here or even that you need to go during regular business hours in order to find them. Many of the ghost sightings here happen from outside on the street. People will glance up to the windows on the third floor and see the silhouette of a man hanging himself. You are more than welcome to look up at those third-floor windows from out in the street all night long, searching for the ghost of the pharmacist's son who hung himself there so many years ago.

MULLIGAN'S IRISH PUB

117 Second Ave. N., Nashville, TN 37201

directions

In the heart of downtown Nashville, just north of Broadway, you'll find Mulligan's. The pub is in a gray, rather nondescript building on the left side of the street if you are walking down Second Avenue from Broadway.

history

Originally called Market Street, Second Avenue has been an important commercial section of the city from its early years all the way to today. Many people have lived, made their living, and passed through this section of Nashville, and it is no wonder that some remnant of those people lives on.

According to many accounts, in the early 1900s a couple lived in the upstairs section of 117 Second Avenue, where Mulligan's is today. The couple was known to be constantly at odds. Their fights could be heard almost constantly from all the way down on the street. The fights were never about one thing in particular but involved anything and everything, and anyone who heard them argue wondered why they were together in the first place.

One day, the woman was found dead at the bottom of the stairs in the area where Mulligan's is now located. She had died during the fall, and since it appeared she had simply fallen down the stairs on her own, the husband was not arrested for her death. Those who had heard them fight night after night, though, always assumed that her husband had shoved her down the stairs.

ghost story

Very strange things seem to happen here at Mulligan's Irish Pub. One story goes that in 1995, a chef at Mulligan's threw away a large platter and went home for the night. The next day the platter was back on the shelf. The chef threw it away again, and it returned again. This happened several more times before the chef decided to smash the dish into small pieces before again discarding it. It returned the next day. Again, he smashed the platter but this time tossed it into the Cumberland River. This time it didn't resurface.

The ghost here seems to dislike change. Whenever something is altered in the building, such as some kind of renovation or staffing change, the employees who open the building in the morning will find chairs and all kinds of other linens and objects on the floor that weren't there the night before. Other times, objects will fling themselves at people who try to change the establishment or hurt it in any way. People who rearrange their table will have their own drink spilled on them. Once an employee had a pan fly at him across the room. Later it was discovered that the employee had been stealing.

Many people think that the ghost is that of the woman who died when she fell down the stairs in the early 1900s. Employees will often see an apparition of a woman standing at the top of the stairs looking down. Sometimes, they will also see the apparition of a menacing man behind her.

visiting

This pub unfortunately went out of business in December 2010. Since the pub was in a historic building on a historic street in downtown, the building itself will not be torn down. There likely will be another business to replace Mulligan's soon. When the new establishment opens, I strongly suggest that you attend the opening. Remember, the ghosts here really don't like change.

PAST PERFECT

122 Third Ave. S., Nashville, TN 37201

directions

Well within the heart of downtown Nashville, Past Perfect sits just a block away from Broadway. If you're following Broadway away from the river, simply turn left onto Third Avenue. Past Perfect will be on your left, less than a block down Third.

history

Near the main strip in downtown Nashville, only about a block away from Broadway, Past Perfect is close enough that a lot of the energy of the strip could affect the restaurant's clientele and atmosphere. Past Perfect itself did not open until 2005, but the building has been around since Nashville's early days. Being so near the heart of the city, the site has been used for shops, bars, and restaurants throughout its lifetime.

There's no telling who the ghost or ghosts here may be.

ghost story

The ghostly activity at the Past Perfect restaurant is mostly confined to two places. The kitchen and the upstairs loft are both reputed to be haunted, and both of these locations tend to have similar ghost stories.

Witnesses to these ghosts will sometimes see shadowy figures throughout the kitchen and loft. Most often, people will glimpse these shadowy figures out of the corner of an eye and will turn to find nothing there. When these figures are investigated in more depth, no one is ever found.

The other occurrence in these two locations is that people will hear strange noises. Pans clanging together, footsteps, laughter, or voices will all be heard, but when these sounds are investigated, no source is ever found.

visiting

The kitchen and the upstairs loft are unfortunately off-limits to the public. This means that the ghostly happenings at Past Perfect are next to impossible for the casual paranormal explorer to experience.

The paranormal activity here is almost exclusively experienced by the restaurant's staff. So, unless you work at the restaurant, you are probably not going to be able to encounter these ghosts. The restaurant is open to the public, however, so you can enter the building and maybe talk with some of the staff about their own experiences with the resident spirits.

PAT'S HERMITAGE CAFE

71 Hermitage Ave., Nashville, TN 37210

directions

Pat's Hermitage Cafe is in downtown Nashville, just south of Broadway. Take Broadway to First Avenue and turn right onto First Avenue. After about four blocks, First Avenue will veer to the left and will change its name to Hermitage Avenue. The cafe will be on the right after four more blocks, at the corner of Hermitage Avenue and Middleton Street.

history

Originally, the Hermitage Cafe was owned by a man named Shields Taylor. Since the restaurant lies on the outskirts of downtown Nashville and is one of the only places that remains open overnight, an eclectic group of patrons has always regularly stopped in. Drunk tourists, construction workers, police officers, and any kind of weird or eccentric person who wants to grab a bite to eat in the middle of the night constantly attend this place. Celebrities have even shown up here from time to time.

In the last few years, Shields Taylor died, leaving the restaurant to his widow, Pat Taylor. The Hermitage Cafe changed its name to Pat's Hermitage Cafe but kept the same hours and eclectic patronage. The cafe was even the setting of Sugarland's video for "Baby Girl."

ghost story

Every ghost story here started after Shields Taylor's death. As soon as he died, though, many people started experiencing ghostly activity in the cafe. This leads many to believe that the ghost here is actually his.

Lots of knocking sounds seem to occur in the building at all hours. There will be violent knocking on the doors even when no one is there. The pots and pans will crash and bang together even though no breeze blows them and no person touches them.

The ghost of Mr. Taylor seems to get a little bolder than these simple sounds, though. Many times, women inside the restaurant have felt someone playing with their hair, but when they turned around they found no one nearby. Other patrons and employees have even been shoved by some unseen force. Perhaps Shields Taylor's personality has left its imprint on the restaurant even after he is gone.

visiting

Pat's Hermitage Cafe has the perfect hours for potential ghosthunters. It is open through the night, opening at 10 p.m. and closing at 1:30 p.m. the next afternoon. Most of the ghostly activity here, as at most locations, happens at night so the hours are perfect. Just head to the cafe during a break in your all-night ghost hunt, and you may just run into a ghost while here.

RED ROSE COFFEE HOUSE AND BISTRO BUILDING

528 W. College St., Murfreesboro, TN 37130

directions

Take I-24 East from the city for about 27 miles. Take Exit 78B, the Old Fort Parkway exit toward Murfreesboro. Follow Old Fort Parkway for 2.5 miles until you reach West College Street. Turn right onto West College Street. The Red Rose Coffee House is no longer in business, but its building will be on your left at the intersection of West College Street and Lytle Street. There is a large wooden deck on the back of the building and decorative painting on the side facing West College Street.

history

Throughout most of the history of this remote corner of Murfreesboro, nothing incredibly momentous or interesting happened. The lot had been empty for a while and eventually became a couple of businesses, most recently the Red Rose Coffee House and Bistro. Finally the Red Rose closed her doors forever and the building continues to sit abandoned.

Perhaps the slice of history most closely related to the ghost here involves a body discovered while the building was still the Red Rose. A deceased homeless man was found in an alley on the Barker Street side of the building.

ghost story

The ghostly things that happen here can easily be attributed to the body that was found in the alley behind the building. When the building was still an operating coffee house, many of the chairs would move by themselves. Drinking glasses and mugs would mysteriously slide off the tables and shatter on the floor. Witnesses would see shadows of people who weren't there and hear voices coming from the empty building.

The ghosts also haunt the building's exterior. Even today, people will witness strange shadows disappearing into the back alley. People will hear footsteps on the deck on the West College Street side. Sometimes visitors will even hear voices or cries coming from the alley but, upon investigation, find no one there.

visiting

The building is abandoned, so it is impossible to gain access to the interior. The windows have been painted over, so it is not even an option to look inside the building. That doesn't mean that this ghost is impossible to experience, though. Many of the ghost stories happen outside the building. You can pull your car into the adjacent lot and explore the area around the empty building.

This would probably not be the best place to visit late at night. Anyone driving by may think it strange that people with flashlights are examining the exterior of an abandoned building, and many times the police don't readily accept the "looking for ghosts" explanation. This is a place that is probably best to explore during the day or near dusk.

RIVERFRONT TAVERN

101 Church St., Nashville, TN 37201

directions

You will find Riverfront Tavern in the heart of downtown Nashville. From Broadway, simply take Second Avenue to the north until you get to Church Street. Turn right onto Church Street, and the Riverfront Tavern will be on your right just past the Beer Sellar.

history

The building that today houses both the Riverfront Tavern and the Beer Sellar (see Beer Sellar chapter) has a very long history. The city began at the river, expanding westward from there. Since the Riverfront Tavern is in a building adjacent to the river and near the center of the city, this building is one of the oldest in Nashville and the site of some of the most historic businesses in the area.

In the city's early history, the area where the tavern is now situated represented an important section of the town. Stores lined all of Second Avenue, then known as Merchant Street. This was a cultural center of the city. In the years of the Civil War, injured from nearby battles would be moved into the downtown area into makeshift hospitals. While the hospitals were centered on Broadway near the current sites of Lawrence Record Shop and Ernest Tubb Record Shop, buildings as far as Second Avenue and Church Street could have been used as hospitals as well.

Today, the area still forms a cultural center of the city, located in the nightclub district which extends down Broadway and Second Avenue, all the way to the intersection with Church Street.

ghost story

The ghost stories here tend toward strange noises and things moving around. Witnesses to the ghostly events here will often hear footsteps throughout the building although no one is walking around. They will hear glasses clinking together and a variety of other knocks and bumps that seem to have no logical explanation.

Other witnesses to the unusual activity will notice items moving around. Glasses will mysteriously glide by themselves across the bar and tables and will sometimes actually fall off and shatter on the floor. Employees will leave something in a specific place and then return to find that the object has somehow been moved to an entirely different area of the tavern.

visiting

Hearing the ghosts here is a lot more difficult than seeing them. This is because you can only enter the bar during normal business hours, and most of the time, it is too loud in the bar to hear anything out of the ordinary. It is entirely possible to simply go to the bar and set your glass on your table, patiently waiting for it to move. You may be surprised when it starts to slide across the table. Just make sure you keep an eye on it; you wouldn't want to be held responsible if it slides off the table and breaks. Riverfront Tavern is open daily from 11 a.m. to 3 a.m.

TOOTSIE'S ORCHID LOUNGE

422 Broadway, Nashville, TN 37201

directions

In the heart of downtown Nashville, Tootsie's purplish façade and bright neon sign make it hard to miss. The lounge is located on Broadway between Fourth and Fifth avenues, just around the corner from the Ryman Auditorium.

history

Entertainer and bar owner Tootsie Bess always had a soft spot for struggling country music artists. In 1960, she purchased the property just around the corner from the

Ryman Auditorium and set it up as a bar and music stage. She called the property "Mom's" until she came in one day to find that the painter she had hired had painted the building an orchid color. From then on she called the place the Orchid Lounge.

Since the lounge was just around the corner from the Ryman, the place where many of the biggest names in country music would often perform, famous people would often stop by Tootsie's before going on stage at the Ryman. Some of these famous artists would actually perform at the lounge, while others would simply watch the acts who were playing and drink a beer.

Tootsie herself was always intent on helping out struggling country music artists. She would hire artists who were down on their luck to play in her lounge. When they were having trouble making their rent or paying their bills, she would slip some extra money into their pockets to help them out. Sometimes, those that she helped would hit it big, and they would always return to repay the favor.

Her funeral was attended by many of the biggest country music celebrities of the time. Country star Connie Smith sang hymns at the funeral as Tootsie was buried in her orchid-colored gown.

ghost story

One of the most prolific ghosts in Nashville, Hank Williams Sr., has apparently made Tootsie's Orchid Lounge his favorite haunt. He is recognized quite often inside the building. Sometimes he is ordering a drink at the bar, and other times he is simply seen in the midst of a crowd of people. People have even run into him in the alley between Tootsie's and Robert's Western World. Those who encounter Old Hank's spirit always report that he is polite.

One appearance that Hank Williams Sr. made at Tootsie's gained national attention when a patron snapped a picture that revealed a white mist on the stage with a face that resembled Old Hank. The strange photo was published in a national magazine.

Hank Williams Sr. isn't the only ghost to haunt this building. People will encounter all types of strange noises and shadowy figures throughout the establishment. Tootsie herself has even made an appearance or two in the building. The story is that Tootsie will appear at the end of the bar whenever there is an act on stage that she likes.

visiting

Tootsie's Orchid Lounge is full-fledged honky-tonk, so you must be 21 years of age to visit. Not only is it open late most nights, the ghosts here are also often seen while the business is open and in full operation. While the smoky atmosphere may make any scientific ghost investigation impossible, it is well worth a trip. Who knows—you might catch a glimpse of a music legend.

SECTION IV

stores and hotels

CONGRESS INN

2914 Dickerson Pike, Nashville, TN 37207

directions

From downtown, take I-65 North about 4 miles to Exit 87, US 431 South/East Trinity Lane. Turn right at the end of the exit onto East Trinity Lane. About a quarter mile down the road, turn left onto Dickerson Pike. Follow Dickerson for a little more than a mile. The Congress Inn will be on the left.

history

Remarkably, this building has been around since the mid-1800s. While you may not think so when looking at it, many people have died here at the Congress Inn. During the Civil War, the area in and around Nashville became a battleground. Thousands of people were killed in battles near Nashville, but dying in these battles was often the easy way to go. Since many of the weapons used during the Civil War were made to inflict maximum damage, if you were wounded and not killed immediately, the remainder of your life was often short and excruciatingly painful.

During the Civil War, the Congress Inn was used as a hospital for wounded soldiers. Dying men were brought here in an attempt to bring them back from the brink of death. Unfortunately, many times it was far too late or the damage far too severe to save these young soldiers. And thus many people died within this building. As the bodies began to build up and those managing the hospital ran out of places to store the deceased, they started burying the dead in the cellar of the building. When the battles stopped and the building ceased to be a hospital, many of those bodies

remained in the basement. According to some rumors, a few of the bodies were even encased within the concrete of the basement walls and never removed for proper burial.

ghost story

In almost every room and hallway of this place, there is some sort of paranormal activity. People will oftentimes encounter unexplainable feelings of discomfort or fear when they are alone in any area of the building. People will report that they are being followed down the hallways by phantom footsteps or they will feel as if they have been touched by some unseen force.

The rooms themselves are reportedly haunted as well. Once, a lodger was sleeping soundly in his room when suddenly he felt as if a large figure had sat upon his legs. He struggled to turn over for several seconds before the invisible figure let him up. Others have reported strange knocks at their doors in the middle of the night or strange feelings of a presence in the room. Perhaps the ghosts of those Civil War soldiers who are still buried in the basement of the main building have taken up residence here.

visiting

There are several positive points to visiting this hotel in hopes of finding its resident ghosts. First of all, the hotel itself is rather inexpensive, less than $40 for an individual room for the night, so it is easy to afford to spend the night in a haunted hotel. Second, the activity is not said to be centered in specific rooms. You can choose to stay in any room and have an equal chance of encountering one of the spirits here.

Your best bet for encountering the ghosts here is within the main building of the hotel, the historic site where most of the activity is reported.

CUZ'S ANTIQUES CENTER

140 Public Square, Lebanon, TN 37087

directions

Take I-40 East for about 29 miles until you reach Exit 238, the US 231 South exit toward Lebanon. At the end of the exit ramp, turn left onto US 231 and follow the road for about 2 miles. At that point, you'll hit the roundabout in the center of the city. Cuz's Antiques Center will be on the right as soon as you turn into the roundabout. There is parking all throughout the area.

history

Cuz's Antiques Center is huge, utilizing three floors in the Public Square in Lebanon to display its wares. All varieties of different items inhabit this store space, and perhaps it is the unique histories of the items in this collection that have led to some of the ghostly activity here. Despite the eclectic and expansive inventory, there are two objects that stand far above the rest in terms of oddity.

The first is a genuine electric chair, which sits in the back of the store. It once sat in a penitentiary in Florida and has actually been used to execute prisoners on death row. It now holds an unassuming spot in the back of the store and is not for sale.

The other item involves the story of a married man and unmarried woman who were once carrying out an affair. They would take his car up to a nearby road called Sugar Flat Road, a popular lovers' lane of the time, where they carried out their illicit relationship. One night, it had gotten quite late and the man insisted that they hurry home. As they sped down Sugar Flat Road, a figure stepped out into the road and the man was unable to stop in time. Thinking that he had hit some animal, he jumped out of the car to look. To his horror, his victim appeared to be some sort of man completely covered with hair. So as not to call attention to his affair, he kept what he had seen a secret from the woman and drove her home and then returned to bury the creature so that he wouldn't get in trouble for it.

When he returned and started burying the creature, he realized that it was one of a kind. He felt that he needed to keep some kind of trophy to prove to himself that the incident had happened. He cut off its head with his shovel and had the head stuffed at a taxidermist. The man's wife didn't like the head on their mantel, so the man had to get rid of it. The head is now on display at Cuz's Antiques Center.

ghost story

There is a large variety of paranormal activity that occurs here due to the vast number of antiques in the building. The most common occurrence is that items will move around throughout the building. Things will fall off shelves as people watch. Items will slide across tables, and people will leave items in one place and then return to find that these items have moved.

People will also hear phantom sounds and voices throughout the building. Footsteps and knocks are heard quite often, and witnesses will also hear voices even when no one else is present.

Witnesses to the paranormal activity here will sometimes also see ghosts. All kinds of full-bodied apparitions have been observed here. Figures that seem to simply be browsing will suddenly vanish into thin air. Other figures will walk straight through walls or displays as if no obstruction is there. On occasion, witnesses will see a shadowy figure out of the corner of an eye. When they turn toward the figure, it has vanished.

visiting

Generally, this building is a fascinating place to visit, but go during business hours. Cuz's is open Monday through Saturday until 5 p.m. The ghosts are most often experienced when people are relatively alone in the store. Early afternoon during the week is probably an ideal time. Catch an employee who isn't busy and ask him or her to point you to the best place to see a ghost.

DILLARD'S AT THE MALL AT GREEN HILLS

2126 Abbott Martin Rd., Ste. 500, Nashville, TN 37215

directions

Take I-440 East to Exit 3, Hillsboro Pike. Turn right onto Hillsboro Pike, and follow this road for a little more than a mile. Turn right at The Mall at Green Hills on Abbott Martin Road. Dillard's is actually inside the mall.

history

This upscale shopping mall may look new and sleek, but it can actually trace its history back to the early 1950s. At that time, the shopping center was actually a strip mall with stores facing the parking lot, and patrons would have to exit one store outside in order to enter another. While Dillard's did not appear at the mall until 1987, the building that Dillard's currently occupies has been around since the mall's creation. Originally, it was a department store called Cain-Sloan.

The Mall at Green Hills didn't become the enclosed mall that it is today until the 1980s, when large-scale renovations began on the original strip mall. By the late 1980s, the structure was completely enclosed, with Dillard's as one of the anchor stores.

The mall's ghosts probably date back to a time long before the strip mall. The area where the mall stands today, just south of Nashville, was traversed by many pioneers in the early days of the city. It is quite likely that pioneers settled in this area around the time that attacks by Native Americans became less frequent and the pioneers depended less on Fort Nashborough.

ghost story

No one would really expect that a place like Dillard's would be haunted, but this particular store does have its own famous ghostly resident. The ghostly activity here is always seen and never heard or felt. Sometimes, people will observe shadow people moving around within the store, but the most famous ghost takes a very specific form.

The ghost appears as a pioneer or Revolutionary War soldier, fully dressed in period clothing and looking very much like someone who has stepped directly from the 1700s into our century. The ghost is always a man who wears a tricornered hat and consistently carries a rifle. If approached or questioned, the ghost disappears.

visiting

This ghost can only be experienced within the store, so you have to enter Dillard's when it is open to the public. The store is open until 9 p.m. every day of the week except Sunday when it closes at 6 p.m. You are most likely to encounter this apparition if you visit the store after nightfall, the time that most of the sightings take place.

The ghosts have been seen in the shoe area of the store, which anyone can visit, so, as an outsider, this would be the best spot to look for the apparition. The place that the apparition is seen most often, though, is in the storeroom of the building. Unfortunately, only employees are permitted in this area.

DRAKE MOTEL

420 Murfreesboro Pike, Nashville, TN 37210

directions

Take Eighth Avenue South from Broadway for about a half mile, and then take a slight left onto Lafayette Street. Follow Lafayette for about 2 miles. Lafayette will change its name to Murfreesboro Pike at the railroad tracks. The Drake Motel will be on your left. The large sign advertising the hotel is difficult to miss.

history

The front entrance to the Drake is graced by a sign that says "Stay Where the Stars Stay." While it may not look like a motel that celebrities are likely to choose, the advertisement isn't entirely false. In the 1930s and 1940s, the Drake Motel was the closest affordable hotel to the Ryman Auditorium. Unknown performers lucky enough to get a gig at the Ryman would stay at the Drake Motel and then sometimes hit it big at the famous country-music concert venue. So many soon-to-be stars would stay at the Drake in those days before they started to find fame that the Drake began billing itself as celebrity lodging.

As the years passed, the Drake became less of a stepping-stone for those people who were on their way to stardom. Since the Grand Ole Opry moved out of the downtown area, the Drake has become more of a motel where tourists would stay if they were looking for affordable lodgings near downtown Nashville.

One day, a lodger who was staying in one of the rooms noticed a strange smell coming from the closet. To the lodger's horror, a body had been stuffed into the closet. When the police came to investigate, they found that the room had initially been completely covered with the murder victim's blood but at some point had been thoroughly cleaned. Upon further investigation they discovered that the maid had actually entered the room the day after the murder, seen the bloody mess, and then cleaned the room for the next lodger. On top of this, she didn't mention to anyone that there was blood all over the room.

The murder is still unsolved.

ghost story

The ghostly happening that occurs most often at the Drake is that people will hear knocking at their door. When they get up to see who is standing at the door, they

find no one. When these witnesses return to bed, the knocking happens again. And again there is no one at the door. At this point the lodger will sometimes wait by the door, hoping that the knock will occur again and that he or she will finally catch the phantom knocker. When the knocking does happen again, they swing the door open immediately, but no one is there.

The ghostly knocking isn't the only thing that people report happening at the Drake. People will get the feeling that they are being watched when alone in their rooms. Occasionally, people staying here will feel someone gently touch their foot in the middle of the night. When they wake up in terror, they see that no one else is in the room.

visiting

You can rent a room at the Drake Motel for less than $50 a night, so it will not break your budget to stay here. Also, when you book a room here for the night, you have the haunted room all to yourself, without worrying about interruptions from others. You can just stay the night in the room, hoping to experience one of the hauntings.

Searching for ghosts at the Drake does not come without some negative points, though. The Drake sits near a not-so-good neighborhood, and sometimes that is reflected in the lodgers who stay at the motel. Tourists have sometimes reported some unsavory characters hanging around near the Drake.

Despite these drawbacks, though, if you want to stay the night in a haunted hotel, this is one of the most affordable options for you in Nashville.

ERNEST TUBB RECORD SHOP

417 Broadway, Nashville, TN 37203

directions

This location is in the heart of downtown Nashville, on Broadway between Fourth and Fifth avenues. A neon sign with a guitar hangs over the sidewalk.

history

While this store is an important fixture in the music scene that has come to define the city of Nashville, it is actually the building's origins in the mid-1800s that have given rise to its ghostly nature.

During the Civil War, Nashville was often a battleground. With its location on several railroad lines and along an important river, the city became an important strategic and psychological prize for both the North and the South during the war. Since so many battles happened within and near Nashville, the city's permanent structures were often used to support the war effort. During much of the fighting near Nashville, the area along what is today Broadway—where the Ernest Tubb Record Shop currently sits—was used as a hospital.

Medicine was still in its infancy during the Civil War, so many people died very painful and prolonged deaths in this hospital. The section of the building currently inhabited by the record shop served as the morgue.

ghost story

The most often reported ghost story here relates to the record shop business. People who are in the record shop during open hours will begin to discuss a certain artist or song, and the very same artist or song will surprisingly begin to play itself on the jukebox that provides the soundtrack for the shop. If this had happened once or twice, it could be easily dismissed as coincidence, but this phenomenon has been reported countless times within the building.

Yet this isn't the only strange thing to happen here. Most of the paranormal activity in the building focuses on the stairs in the back of the shop. People, especially employees, will often report cold or hot spots in certain areas on the stairs, where there is a markedly different temperature from the rest of the building.

Others within the building have mentioned feelings of discomfort, as if they are being watched. Still others report being touched gently on the shoulder but turning and seeing no one there.

visiting

The building is accessible during regular business hours, and, as a result, this is the best time to go to search for ghosts. For your best chance to experience the strange phenomena here, enter the store and begin talking about a particular artist or song and see if the jukebox begins to play that music. The record shop is open Sunday through Wednesday, 9 a.m. to 10 p.m.; Thursday, 9 a.m. to 11 p.m.; and Friday and Saturday, 9 a.m. to midnight.

If you are unable to get to the building during business hours, its interior is still visible from the street. Because its front consists of glass windows, one can easily see into the building. Some people have been touched or have felt watched when they gaze into the building from the outside.

FATE SANDERS MARINA

3157 Weakley Ln., Mount Juliet, TN 37122

directions

Take I-24 East for 15 miles until you get to Exit 66B, Sam Ridley Parkway West toward Smyrna. Follow this road for another 5 miles, and then turn left onto Weakley Lane. Follow Weakley Lane for another 4 miles. The marina will be on your left.

history

Hidden in a cove on Percy Priest Lake near Smyrna, Fate Sanders Marina has been a favorite place for boaters for several years now. The marina has a restaurant, tackle shop, and boat rentals for anyone interested in going out on the lake.

The darker history of the area doesn't involve the marina itself as much as the lake immediately adjacent. Once a boy went out with his father on a boat on Percy Priest Lake and fell off the boat into the water. The boy was not wearing a life vest and was somehow sucked under the water. His father dove from the boat into the water, doing all he could to save his child and searching desperately for him, but the boy's body was never found.

ghost story

The ghost of the boy who drowned in the lake haunts the Fate Sanders Marina to this day. Many times, people who see the boy will not even realize that he is a ghost. The boy will walk up to someone at the marina and ask the person if he or she has seen his father. Not knowing who the boy is, witnesses will say that they haven't seen the boy's father and the boy will move on, supposedly to ask another the same question.

Sometimes, people will offer to help the poor boy find his father at the marina. When this happens, the ghost will usually mysteriously disappear, and the witness will begin to wonder if the child was ever even there in the first place.

visiting

When visiting, keep in mind that the marina area opens at 6 a.m. every day of the week (it is closed during five holidays during the year) and closes at 9 p.m. every day except Friday and Saturday when it closes at 10 p.m. There is nothing stopping you from entering the marina during these times to look for the little boy. The restaurant, tackle shop, and boat rentals are open to the public, so the best way to perhaps encounter the ghost would be to hang around these places and hope that the boy decides to ask you to help find his father.

GAYLORD OPRYLAND RESORT AND CONVENTION CENTER

2800 Opryland Dr., Nashville, TN 37214

directions

Only 17 minutes from downtown, simply take Seventh Avenue North to Charlotte Avenue. Turn left onto Charlotte Avenue, and it will soon become James Robertson Parkway. Take the ramp onto US 31 East North/Ellington Parkway, and follow this road for about 5 miles until the TN 155 East/Briley Parkway exit. Follow TN 155 East toward Opryland until you reach Exit 12, McGavock Pike West. Merge onto Music Valley Drive. You will take your first right and then your first left to reach the parking lot of the Opryland Resort.

history

While the hotel itself is a spectacular work of architecture and design, it would be remiss to mention the hotel without first mentioning the surrounding area. Since 1925, the Grand Ole Opry has been broadcasting a country music radio show. It is the goal of any country music star to appear on this program. Since the stage at the Grand Ole Opry became such a mecca for country music fans near and far, in 1972

Gaylord Entertainment decided that they would build an amusement park called Opryland adjacent to the Grand Ole Opry stage. Because the area attracted so many tourists from across the country, the next logical step was to build a hotel near these two destinations. In 1977, Gaylord built a hotel and called it the Opryland Hotel.

And what a hotel it has become. Over the years it has grown into one of the grandest hotels in the world. It is the largest hotel in America that doesn't include a casino. In fact, with 2,881 rooms, it is the largest hotel in the country outside of Las Vegas. It features a large tropical garden inside the building, fueled by the sun shining through the building's expansive glass ceiling. Many of the hotel's rooms have balconies which overlook the gardens. There are 14 retail stores, 14 restaurants, a nightclub, and a spa all within the walls of this immense hotel.

The flood of May 2010 did immense damage to the hotel when the waters of the adjacent Cumberland River rushed over the banks and into the hotel. Much of the hotel was underneath 5–10 feet of water, forcing the building to close down until late 2010.

ghost story

As at any large hotel, a vast variety of ghostly encounters has been reported over the years. Most of the activity here seems to occur late at night, during the third shift when most of the corridors are empty and most of the stores are closed. People will

often experience uneasiness and will feel as though they are being followed although no one is around. People will sometimes hear voices and will be unable to pinpoint their source. When walking around the massive hotel late at night, many people are simply uncomfortable, and some attribute the feeling to the presence of one of the hotel's many ghosts.

While many of the building's ghosts represent merely feelings that stem from unseen forces, at least one ghost here is often seen throughout the building. When walking alone through one of the building's many corridors or paths, people will often come across the ghost of a woman dressed in clothing from the mid-1900s. Sometimes she will be following employees or residents down the corridor and then will simply vanish without a trace. Other times, witnesses will approach her, and she will suddenly disappear before their eyes. Most employees of the building have either seen the ghost or know the stories about her. They call her Mrs. McGavock after a wealthy local woman who played a part in establishing the area as a country music landmark.

visiting

The biggest obstacle in visiting the Opryland Resort if you are not renting a room for the night is quite simply parking. It costs $18 to park at the hotel. Luckily, there is parking at the adjacent mall and Grand Ole Opry Theater. The walk is long from that lot, but often preferable to the $18 parking fee.

Once you access the resort, you can roam around as much as you'd like. Try to find one of the more remote corners of the building since this is where the ghostly activity occurs most often. Of course the easiest way to find a ghost here is to actually rent a room for the night and explore your room and the hotel throughout your stay, but the rooms here are quite expensive and such an endeavor may go beyond many ghosthunters' budgets.

LAWRENCE RECORD SHOP

409 Broadway, Nashville, TN 37203

directions

Lawrence Record Shop is in the heart of downtown Nashville, on Broadway near its intersection with Fourth Avenue. You'll see a large sign facing the street above the storefront. The shop is on the same side of the road and same block as the Ernest Tubb Record Shop and across the street from Tootsie's Orchid Lounge.

history

The Lawrence Record Shop is one of the most famous and oldest record shops in the city of Nashville. The shop has been around for almost 60 years and has followed the development of the country music genre that has given Nashville its reputation as Music City. While originally, the shop only sold vinyl records, over the years it has developed with the times. It now encompasses all four floors of the building it inhabits and has a phenomenal selection of all types of music.

The ghosts are probably here because of a few nuggets of history about this place. The building itself has been around since the mid-1800s and was used as a Civil War hospital during the Battle of Nashville and other nearby battles during the war. Many people suffered and likely died here. The record store next door, Ernest Tubb Record Shop (see Ernest Tubb Record Shop chapter), was actually used as a morgue since the basement there was cooler than street level.

When the Lawrence Record Shop first came into business in the mid-1900s, Mr. Lawrence himself would usually be at the shop throughout the day. Until the day he died, he smoked cigars and would often be seen smoking them while greeting his customers inside his record shop.

ghost story

Right after Mr. Lawrence died, odd things started occurring inside his store. Many of these strange things still happen to this day. One paranormal incident that occurs quite often inside the Lawrence Record Shop involves a very distinct phantom smell that has lingered here for many years. Customers will sometimes complain that it smells like cigar smoke inside the building. Often they will bring their concerns to the employees, telling them that it smells as if someone has been smoking a cigar in the building. The employees will inform the customers that there is absolutely no smoking allowed inside the building but will secretly know that Mr. Lawrence is present from beyond the grave.

Other witnesses to the paranormal will sometimes hear phantom footsteps throughout the building, especially when they are on one of the upper floors alone. They look for the source of the footsteps and are unable to find anything.

visiting

The Lawrence Record Shop is open from Tuesday until Saturday from 11 a.m. to 5:30 p.m. The shop is closed on Sunday and Monday. You would need to enter the store during normal business hours in order to experience the ghostly activity here, since it occurs exclusively inside the building. You are most likely to find a ghost here if you climb to one of the upper floors of the building. These floors are typically more isolated and are where people experience the ghostly smells and footsteps most often.

LEBANON PREMIUM OUTLETS
1 Outlet Village Blvd., Lebanon, TN 37090

directions
Take I-40 East toward Knoxville for about 29 miles. Get off at Exit 238 toward Lebanon/Hartsville, and turn right at the end of the ramp onto US 231. The outlet mall will be on your right about a quarter mile down the road. The sign is clearly visible from the highway.

history
The Lebanon Premium Outlets looks so sleek and contemporary that it's hard to believe it is reputed to be haunted. The mall itself is relatively new, and the area surrounding it is not drenched in any kind of regional history. The land where it sits had always just been farmland, and there is no record of anyone dying on the property.

ghost story
Hauntings here seem to be caused by two different ghosts, and both of them seem to be the ghosts of older people who, for some reason, still walk through these retail establishments.

The most often seen ghost is that of an old woman who is frequently encountered at the food court. People will be minding their own business while eating in the food court when an older woman unexpectedly approaches and greets them. The woman appears so real and tangible that no one gives her a second thought, until abruptly she vanishes. As much as the witnesses try to convince themselves that she had somehow slipped away from them unseen, they can never relocate her. Several different customers have reported seeing the same old woman who greets them and then vanishes suddenly and without a trace.

The other ghost that is seen at the outlet mall is a little less localized and somewhat rarer. As closing time approaches, an old man will enter a store (the phantom will materialize in many different stores throughout the mall, not willing to limit himself to a single establishment) and quietly mumble something to an employee as he passes and disappears into the deeper recesses of the building. When the employee follows to inform him that the store is closing, he or she is unable to find anyone anywhere in the store. The old man is simply no longer there.

visiting

The ghost encounters here have both positive and negative aspects. First, for the positives, both ghosts are seen only while the mall is open, so you have no problems gaining access to the area that these ghosts are said to haunt. Second, the ghost of the old woman is limited to a very small area: the dining area at the food court. If you are looking for that ghost, you don't need to do anything but grab a bite to eat at the food court and then sit back and wait. According to the story, she will come and greet you. The third advantage is that, if you are interested in finding the old man's ghost, you know when to go looking for him. The ghost of the old man is always seen near closing time, 9 p.m.

One detriment to finding the ghost of the old woman is that there is no specific time of day that she chooses to appear. She could show up at any moment from the time the mall opens at 10 a.m. to the time it closes at 9 p.m. Yet an even bigger obstacle perhaps stands in the way of encountering the ghost of the old man. While he seems to materialize at the same time of the day, he likes to travel from store to store. It is impossible to tell which store he may walk into on any given day, so if you were to visit a store near closing time in hopes of seeing him, it is the luck of the draw as to whether you choose the right store.

ROBERT'S WESTERN WORLD

416B Broadway, Nashville, TN 37203

directions

Robert's Western World lies in the heart of downtown Nashville. It is on Broadway between Fourth and Fifth avenues on the same side of the road as Tootsie's Orchid Lounge and across the street from Ernest Tubb Record Shop and the Lawrence Record Shop.

history

For the past 11 years, Robert's Western World has been a favorite honky-tonk in the heart of downtown Nashville. The area where it sits, however, in the shadow of the Ryman Auditorium, has been a mecca for country music fans for most of the last century. Country music's greats have certainly walked the area and entered the building where Robert's is today.

Before it was a honky-tonk, and even to an extent today, Robert's was a store that sold western apparel and cigars. You could buy anything from boots to lighters here.

Today, the building is more a bar than a store and they present live music every day and every night.

ghost story

The ghosts at Robert's Western World are most often experienced by employees who are opening up the place for the day or closing it down for the night. These employees will hear strange noises throughout the building. Knocks will sound for no reason. Footsteps will be heard when no one is there. All varieties of metallic sounds will clank though no source for these sounds is ever found.

The employees will also see strange lights throughout the building when they are opening or closing. Balls of light will inexplicably float through the air. Lights will turn on and off for no reason.

One of Nashville's most prolific ghosts, Hank Williams Sr. (see Tootsie's Orchid Lounge and Ryman Auditorium chapters), will from time to time make an appearance at Robert's Western World. Witnesses will report that he appears white and misty. The ghost will dissipate and slowly vanish as the flabbergasted onlookers watch.

visiting

If you're coming here to see the resident ghosts, one of the obvious pitfalls is that they are seen or heard most often before the building opens to the public and after it closes. This makes ghostly encounters here next to impossible for someone who doesn't work here. Yet these ghosts have also been reported by customers who are the first to come or the last to leave. Perhaps these ghosts are here all the time but become more obvious when the hustle and bustle of the business day dies down.

Robert's opens at 11 a.m. Monday through Saturday and at noon on Sunday. It closes at 3 a.m. every day of the week. Strangely, Robert's also has a Sunday morning Gospel Fellowship at 10:30 a.m. that invites people to come and worship.

UNION STATION HOTEL

1001 Broadway, Nashville, TN 37203

directions

Rising high above the structures around it, this building is hard to miss on the west side of Nashville. It is actually on Broadway itself, on the western edge of downtown at the 10th Avenue intersection. The immense clock tower, topped by a golden statue of the Roman god Mercury, is the building's most recognizable feature.

history

In 1900, Nashville decided to build a Union Station to bring the city's eight different railroad companies together under one roof. One day in 1918, the station was running at full capacity when a train left the station at around 7:07 a.m. Unbeknownst to those on board, another train was running a half hour late and was heading toward Nashville. The two trains collided just to the west of the Union Station (see Dutchman's Curve chapter). One hundred and one people were killed in the tragedy, making it the deadliest train wreck in American history. Many of the dead and wounded were transported back to the Union Station, where the baggage claim area, today the Flying

Saucer bar (see Flying Saucer chapter), was used as a temporary morgue and many of the platforms were turned into temporary hospitals.

After the tragedy, business continued as normal, peaking during World War II as many young men from Tennessee boarded trains on their way to war. After WWII and the advent of the Interstate Highway System, train travel became less popular and the Union Station eventually fell into disuse. In October of 1979, the building was abandoned completely.

Viewing the building as a landmark, Nashville natives were unwilling to let the structure be demolished. A group of investors came up with an idea to turn the building into a hotel in the early 1980s, but it wasn't until 1998 that their plan finally came to fruition. While the building is a hotel today, for almost 20 years the immense structure lay completely abandoned.

ghost story

One of the more famous ghosts here is that of a young man who is wearing a WWII-era military uniform. The story goes that the man departed from this train station during WWII and was killed in battle. Since he left his family and loved ones at this station, he has returned here in an attempt to find them again.

Another ghost is supposedly that of a woman who fell from a platform and was torn apart by an approaching train. This ghost appears very much as the woman may have looked in the aftermath of the accident. She is completely covered in blood and is sometimes missing her right arm and part of her face.

Some of the hotel rooms themselves are haunted as well, especially those on the fifth floor. People will hear loud banging sounds in the middle of the night and electrical accessories in the room like lamps and televisions will turn on and off by themselves.

visiting

The hotel is actually quite upscale and expensive, so be prepared to spend a lot of money if you are interested in staying the night. There is a restaurant inside the building, so you don't necessarily have to stay the night at the haunted hotel in order to enter the building, though the restaurant is rather expensive as well. If you are interested in the building and are exploring on a low budget, your best bet may be to just admire the haunted structure from the outside.

WALKING HORSE HOTEL

101 Spring St., Wartrace, TN 37183

directions

Take I-24 East for about 45 miles until you reach Exit 97, the TN 64 exit. Turn right onto TN 64, and follow that road for about 9 miles until you get to Spring Street. Turn right onto Spring Street, and the Walking Horse Hotel will be at the intersection on your left.

history

The historical importance of this building is due more to an animal than any person. The Walking Horse Hotel was famous in its day, and is still remembered because of a single horse that was stabled here. The horse, known as Strolling Jim, is famous because he became the first world champion Tennessee walking horse in 1939.

The building itself was built in 1912, but it wasn't until the late 1930s that Strolling Jim and his trainer, Floyd Carothers, began to utilize the building. After the championship in 1939, Strolling Jim traveled around the world competing and exhibiting. Finally, in 1947, Strolling Jim came back to Wartrace and to the Walking Horse Hotel and spent the rest of his life here. He was buried on the premises, and his headstone is still displayed proudly on the property.

Over the decades that followed, the building began to decay and fall into some disrepair, until a man named Joe Peters purchased and restored the building in 2007. During renovation, his wife tragically passed away from cancer. The auditorium here is named after her.

ghost story

Many ghost stories circulate about this building. Some of these stories are ones ghost enthusiasts are used to hearing. Visitors commonly experience feelings of discomfort in the building. Strange shadowy figures will move through the hallways. People will hear strange whispers and footsteps, and unexplained voices and sounds will mysteriously come up on recordings. A white glowing apparition will float up and down the main stairway.

Other ghost stories about this building are a little more unusual and are possibly unique to this place. While owner Joe Peters insists that these stories are nothing more than Internet fabrications, many stories proliferate about a phantom horse that walks throughout the bottom floor of the hotel. The horse is white and transparent and walks through the building as if it weren't there. Those who have seen it report that it looks like a projected movie of a horse walking through a wall and out the other side.

The guest rooms on the third floor are also reportedly haunted by the ghost of trainer Floyd Carothers, whose room was on this floor during the time he spent here. People will run into an apparition that they recognize from photos of Carothers.

visiting

Undoubtedly, the easiest way to experience the ghosts here at the Walking Horse Hotel is to spend the night. There are only six rooms available for rent, but since the reports of paranormal activity here are so frequent, this is probably the most favorable option for experiencing these ghosts.

For those who do not wish to spend the whole night, there are other ways to gain admittance into the building. You might catch a live performance at the music hall here, or you could grab a bite to eat in the onsite restaurant.

The hotel is proud of their ghosts and, if they have the opportunity, employees will happily speak with anyone about them. Feel free to stop in to ask about their ghosts.

ZIERRA MYST

12020 Lebanon Rd., Ste. A, Mount Juliet, TN 37122

directions

Travel along I-40 East from the city for a little more than 11 miles to Exit 221A, the Old Hickory Boulevard exit. Take Old Hickory Boulevard/TN 45 North for about 3 miles until you reach Lebanon Pike. Veer right onto Lebanon Pike, and follow the road for 6 miles. The road will change its name to Lebanon Road, and Zierra Myst will be on the right.

history

The Zierra Myst store has not been at this location for very long. It is a relatively new metaphysical store that specializes in items that "cater to all religions." They sell books, crystals, herbs, incense, jewelry, oils, and art. On top of this, they do psychic and astrological readings as well as hypnosis and weddings. The spells and magic that are performed in the building may account for some of the paranormal activity that occurs here.

If the ghosts do not bear responsibility for the peaceful metaphysical atmosphere of this place, it may have something to do with the land on which the building was constructed. The area was heavily populated with Native Americans in the time before Europeans settled in Tennessee. Perhaps the ghosts are remnants of some lost piece of history from that time.

ghost story

You may be surprised to hear that Carol Humphrey, the owner of Zierra Myst, hasn't experienced many ghostly happenings here in the building, but she has reported some things that strike her as strange. A couple times, she has placed certain items in specific places but later returned to find that the items have been moved to completely different areas of the store.

The more unusual paranormal occurrences have been reported by several different patrons who have come into the store. The store seems to be haunted by the apparitions of three older Native American women. Patrons in the store will sometimes suddenly turn to notice these three Native Americans. As the witnesses are looking at them, the three women immediately disappear as if they were never there in the first place.

visiting

In order to visit these ghosts at the Zierra Myst store, you will probably need to visit during regular business hours. While it is certainly possible that these ghosts could appear to people walking by the store after closing and looking into its glassfront doors, up to this point no one has ever seen them after close. This shouldn't dissuade you from going to search for them, though. The store is open during the week from 10:30 a.m. to 8 p.m. and on Saturday until 5:30 p.m. The store has a great, tranquil atmosphere that makes anyone who enters feel welcome. Walk on in to browse or to buy, and maybe you'll come across three Native American spirits—perhaps there for the same reason.

Union Station Hotel, see page 136

SECTION V

roads and parks

ADAMS RAILROAD CROSSING

Murphy Street, Adams, TN 37010

directions

Take I-65 North to I-24 West, and follow that for a little more than 25 miles to Exit 19, the TN 256 North exit toward Adams. Follow this road for about 8 miles, and then turn left onto Cedar Hill Road. After another 2.5 miles, turn right onto South Commerce Street. Take the first right onto Murphy Street. The haunted railroad tracks will be only a short distance down the road.

history

The entire area in and around Adams contains many ancient Native American burial mounds. Many of these mounds were destroyed to make room for development. Primarily residential homes and farmland took over the site of the now-flattened mounds, though many of the mounds also fell victim to the railroad tracks that cross through Adams. One such mound was supposedly in the area where the tracks cross Murphy Street.

A story tells about a railroad worker who was carrying a lantern and walking along the tracks late at night in the area near what is today Murphy Street. Somehow, he became stuck to the tracks as an oncoming train rocketed toward him. He was unable to move in time and was decapitated by the train.

ghost story

There are stories of dark, shadowy figures that walk the tracks in this area, only to mysteriously disappear when approached or when light shines directly at them.

But the more popular ghost story connected to this area tells of a mysterious light often seen on the tracks near the intersection. Witnesses claim that the light looks like an old lantern being carried by someone down the tracks. The light will bob up and down slightly as it moves either toward or away from the intersection. Legend says that this is the ghost of the railroad man who was decapitated here. He carries the lantern at night looking for his missing head.

visiting

Only the surrounding neighborhood is an obstacle when looking for ghosts at this location. The tracks are closely bordered on all sides by a nice, quiet residential neighborhood. Any of the people in these houses would almost certainly wonder why someone was out on the railroad tracks in the middle of the night and may approach you or call the authorities if you linger on or around the tracks. Of course, it is always dangerous to stop for any reason on railroad tracks that are still in use.

This being said, your best bet for witnessing the ghosts here is to stop your car for a short time near the tracks, at a place that allows you to still see a reasonable distance down the tracks and look for the light. If you don't see any lights for the first minute or two, it would probably be advisable to simply move on.

CENTENNIAL PARK

2600 West End Ave., Nashville, TN 37203

directions

Near downtown Nashville, to get here from the heart of the city, simply take Broadway away from the river for about 2 miles. Along the way, Broadway will change its name to West End Avenue. Centennial Park will be a large park on your right about 2 miles from the river.

history

The Tennessee Centennial and International Exposition was a world's fair held west of downtown in the area that today is Centennial Park. The city hosted the fair in 1897 in order to celebrate the centennial of Tennessee's statehood. Twenty-one temporary buildings were constructed for the fair, and the land itself was turned into beautiful fairgrounds. When the fair ended, the land was to be sold off to the public, but Percy Warner, a park official in Nashville, purchased most of the property to turn it into a permanent park. He was able to attain the land with the Parthenon, a reconstruction of the Greek landmark meant to celebrate Nashville as the "Athens of the West," and the pond. In 1903, this became the first public park in Nashville.

Some dark history lingers at the park, such as the murder of a homeless man and a handful of other deaths including at least one suicide and the only Nashville fatality during the 1998 tornado outbreak. Yet these deaths don't seem to be the driving force behind the paranormal activity here. Many strange occurrences and rituals have happened and continue to happen in the park.

At the corner of 25th Avenue and Elliston Place, there is a funeral home that seems to be situated on the park's land. The land where the funeral home now sits was purchased at about the time that Percy Warner was buying up the rest of the land, and it slipped away from him and the park. The owners of the funeral home were rather eccentric and were into spiritualism and the paranormal. During one séance, they managed to summon a creature that would run around the feet of those gathered, untying shoes and removing socks. When the original owner of the house died, his funeral ceremony was held at midnight in secret and was supposedly attended by many high-ranking Freemasons.

The Parthenon is often the meeting place of many pagans in the area and from across the continent. Offerings will sometimes be left by curiously dressed witches and pagans at the Parthenon's statues.In July of 2009, 27 birds, hundreds of fish, and hundreds of snails abruptly died in and around the pond within Centennial Park. The Department of Agriculture tested the animals' remains and could find no reason that they all suddenly dropped dead.

ghost story

Some of the ghost stories at Centennial Park seem as peculiar as some of the true stories here. People will see strange fires burning within the park and then will investigate and find nothing there. People will observe apparitions in the park. Sometimes the apparitions appear as normal humans and then mysteriously vanish; but other times, the apparitions will be much more bizarre. People will see lion and elephant apparitions in the park as well as other mysterious creatures that cannot be identified. These apparitions vanish when approached. There is even an account of a ghostly plane with angel wings that has been seen in the park.

In the section of the park near the funeral home, people have felt something like a cat rubbing against their ankles. When they look down to see what is at their feet, there is nothing there. Sometimes these hapless victims find that their shoes have been untied.

visiting

The park is open until 11 p.m. every day, and admission and parking are free. This means that, especially during the fall and winter, you have several hours of darkness during which to explore the park. The park is reasonably safe, but I wouldn't go into some dark corner alone.

CHAPEL HILL GHOSTLIGHTS

Depot Street, Chapel Hill, TN 37034

directions

Take I-65 South from the city for about 23 miles until you reach Exit 59A. Take TN 840 East toward Knoxville/Murfreesboro for about 4.5 miles to Exit 34, Peytonsville Trinity Road. Turn right onto Peytonsville Trinity Road, and then take your first left onto Peytonsville Arno Road. Follow this road for about 2 miles, and then turn right onto Arno Allisona Road. Follow Arno Allisona Road for a little more than 6 miles until you reach the Horton Highway. Turn right onto the highway and travel that road for 8.5 miles until you reach Broadview Street. Turn right, and take the second left onto Lawrence Avenue. Once on Lawrence Avenue, take your second right onto Depot Street and continue to the railroad crossing. The road goes both over and under the tracks. You will have to go over the tracks in order to see the ghost light. Do not exit your car onto the tracks, or you will be arrested. The ghost light is most often seen down the stretch of tracks near the water tower.

history

Everyone has a similar story about what happened on these tracks. Legend has it that a railroad worker was walking here late at night carrying a very bright lantern. It was raining heavily, and the terrain was wet and slick. As the railroad worker stepped into an exceptionally deep puddle, he tripped and fell to the ground, knocking his head upon one of the steel rails. He was knocked unconscious and did not awaken even as a train bore down on him. Though the man was visible because of his bright lantern, the train was unable to stop in time.

As the train's brakes squealed in an unsuccessful attempt at stopping, it rolled over him, instantly decapitating him. In the bloody aftermath of the accident, most of the man's body was recovered, but no matter how long the authorities looked, the head could not be found.

ghost story

Walking the tracks in the same area where he was killed, the deceased railroad worker reportedly still searches for his lost head.

This is one of the most famous ghost stories not only in Tennessee but in the entire country. People will oftentimes see a light bouncing up and down along the tracks. The light will look very much like a lantern being carried down the tracks, which leads many to the conclusion that it is the man who was killed there.

The ghost lights are seen so frequently that there are other theories as to their origin. Since the ghost lights are often observed on the same night as UFO activity in the area, some people have suggested that the Chapel Hill lights have something to do with alien spacecraft. Others have looked for scientific explanations or lighting illusions but have come up with nothing.

visiting

Whatever you do, do not step onto the tracks. The tracks are the property of the railroad and the management will prosecute you to the fullest extent of the law if you are caught on the property. Beyond this, the area is patrolled very diligently by local law enforcement. Even if you step out of your car near the tracks, you will be approached by the police and possibly arrested or fined for trespassing. They do not do this because they have anything against ghosthunters, but rather because many people who are searching for the lights have been involved in train accidents or delays. They are very serious about these rules, so no matter what you see stay off the tracks.

This doesn't necessarily mean that the ghost lights are impossible to witness now. There is a public road that crosses the tracks, And when you cross the tracks on this road, you can look down the tracks for the ghost light. However, one stipulation with this strategy is that you cannot stop on the tracks. Remaining on the tracks is again very dangerous and should be avoided at all costs. If you want to see the famous Chapel Hill ghost lights, your only option is to drive over the tracks, looking for the lights down the tracks as you do so. The best area to look is the area near the water tower.

DEAD MAN'S CURVE AT DEMONBREUN

Demonbreun Street and 16th Avenue South,
Nashville, TN 37203

directions

This dead man's curve is located in a roundabout just west of downtown Nashville.
Simply take Broadway away from the river until you reach 16th Avenue. Turn left onto
16th Avenue, and follow the road for about two blocks until you hit the roundabout.
The haunted area surrounds the roundabout. There is a large statue of several naked
people in the center of the traffic circle.

history

Before the construction of the roundabout at the corner of Demonbreun Street and
16th Avenue, there was a sharp curve in the road known to Nashvillians as Dead
Man's Curve. The curve in the road gained its ominous name because of the way it
would sneak up on unsuspecting motorists. Many of these drivers traveling through

the area would not notice how sharp the turn was and would end up being unable to navigate it at the speed they were going.

Throughout the many years that this Dead Man's Curve existed, countless car and motorcycle accidents occurred here. While many of the accidents resulted only in damaged vehicles and minor injuries, some did actually cause fatalities, especially when the vehicle that had crashed was a motorcycle.

As Nashville began to grow and the Music Row district of the city became bigger, the city decided to change the road. The dangerous curve became a roundabout, and a large statue was constructed in its center. The roundabout was named Buddy Killen Circle after an important country music star.

ghost story

Fortunately, the dangerous curve itself no longer exists. The memories of many of the dark things that occurred here seem to still echo in the area though. People will often encounter apparitions walking in and around Buddy Killen Circle long after dark. Many times, these apparitions are simply dark, shadowy figures that will suddenly disappear when approached. Sometimes these figures are simply standing still, and sometimes they walk from one side of the circle to another.

There have been reports of a phantom hitchhiker who haunts the roundabout at Demonbreun. There will be a dark, shadowy figure in the roundabout that extends his thumb, waiting for a motorist to pick him up. Whenever a driver stops for the figure, the ghost mysteriously vanishes. The hitchhiker does not have any features on his face or body. He will often appear as more of a shadow than a real person.

visiting

Even though there is no longer a curve at Demonbreun and 16th, it is still possible to encounter the ghosts here. The most productive way to find these ghosts is to drive your car through the area between 2 and 4 a.m. For some reason, this is the time of night that most people see these shadowy figures and the phantom hitchhiker.

The roundabout is open throughout the night and is not very busy during these early-morning hours. You can spend the whole night driving through this roundabout if you like, and it would be completely legal.

DUTCHMAN'S CURVE

10 White Bridge Pike, Nashville, TN 37205

directions

Negotiating this route will entail both driving and walking. Take I-40 West to I-440 East, Exit 206 on the left side of the highway. Follow I-440 East for a little less than a mile and a half and exit at Exit 1A, US 70S West. Follow this road for a little more than a mile and a half, and then turn right onto White Bridge Pike. Immediately after crossing the bridge, there will be a small parking area on your right just past the train tracks and near a historical marker for the Dutchman's Curve train wreck. At the end of the parking area is a paved trail. You'll have to follow this trail for about a quarter mile until you reach a small area with train wreckage and the remnants of an old bridge. A small sign describing the train wreck will tell you that you are in the right place.

history

At shortly after 7 a.m. on July 9, 1918, the No. 4 train left Union Station in Nashville heading westbound toward Memphis. The conductor of the No. 4 was warned that an incoming train, the No. 1 from Memphis, was running about 35 minutes behind schedule. The No. 4 was instructed to make sure that they were passed by the No. 1 before they started upon the 10 miles of track that is shared by east- and westbound traffic.

The conductor heard a train pass as he was collecting tickets and assumed that it was the No. 1. When he reached the convergence of the tracks at Shops Junction, the tower operator gave him the go-ahead. As the No. 4 entered the single track, the tower operator realized the mistake. He wired the dispatcher that No. 1 had not yet signed in. Dispatch immediately wired back, "He meets No. 1 there, can you stop him?" The tower operator sounded the emergency whistle, but the No. 4 was too far out to hear it.

Just past White Bridge Pike at a gentle curve in the tracks called Dutchman's Curve, the No. 4 was moving at around 50 mph westbound and the No. 1 was moving at about 60 mph eastbound. By the time the two trains saw one another, it was far too

late. The trains collided head-on, sending the wooden passenger cars flying out into the nearby fields. The wreck could be heard for two miles.

News of the accident quickly spread, and people from all over the area rushed to help the survivors. Fifty thousand people came to the scene in order to help. Many of the bodies and injured were transported back along the tracks to the Union Station (see Union Station Hotel chapter). When all was said and done, at least 101 people were killed in the wreck. This makes it the deadliest train wreck in American history.

The conductor of the inbound No. 1 train was killed in the accident. He was set to retire upon reaching Nashville.

ghost story

Ghostly sounds are often heard at the site where the two trains collided at Dutchman's Curve. While haunted places generally tend to have all varieties of ghostly activity, the ghost stories are limited to sounds here. When witnesses stand near the place where the accident happened, they will sometimes hear the sounds of squealing train brakes. Other times, people will hear screams and sounds that resemble people moaning or crying out in agony. These sounds will happen both during daylight hours and at night, but most often early in the morning, around the time that the train accident actually occurred.

visiting

Only during daylight hours are you permitted on the trail leading to the site of the wreck, so you shouldn't go out there at night as you may be arrested for trespassing. This is OK, though, because the sounds are heard most often around 7:20 a.m., the time when the actual train accident occurred. Make sure you bring your recorder in case you do hear the ghosts.

Keep in mind a couple other points for your safety on the trail. The area is prone to flash floods, so do not go out on the trail in the aftermath of any significant rainstorm. Also, it would be safest to bring someone with you. The site of the wreck is rather remote, and you wouldn't want to be caught out here alone with no one to help you if anything were to happen.

EDWIN WARNER PARK

50 Vaughn Rd., Nashville, TN 37221

directions

Use I-40 West for 9 miles until you reach Exit 199, the Old Hickory Boulevard exit. At the end of the exit, turn left onto Old Hickory Boulevard and follow this road for about 4 miles. At this point, it will seem that Old Hickory Boulevard dead-ends into TN 100, but it actually continues. Turn left onto TN 100, and then take your first right onto the continuation of Old Hickory Boulevard. Take your first right onto Vaughn Road, which takes you into Edwin Warner Park.

history

Together Edwin Warner Park and Percy Warner Park are considered the largest municipal park in the state of Tennessee. The land was donated by the Warner family, several members of which were important park commissioners for Nashville in the late 1800s. It took until 1930 before the layout of both parks was completed.

Since 1941, the parks have played host to the Iroquois Steeplechase horse race. The race is the only such race in the entire state that is not run on level ground. In 1984, the parks were added to the National Register of Historic Places and are to this day well kept and beautiful.

ghost story

In the 1950s and 1960s, Edwin Warner Park became a popular lover's lane among the teenagers in the area. Many local teens would seek out the solitary corners of the park to stop their car and "make out.". As the park became increasingly well known as a lover's lane, a strange story began to pop up again and again.

The story goes that a murderer had escaped from a local insane asylum. The murderer had somehow lost his right hand at some point during his life and had it replaced by a hook. As the rumors began to circulate around the neighborhood near Edwin Warner Park about the escaped mental patient, teenagers in the area at dark began to report seeing the man. The couples would be busy in their cars when they would hear metal scraping along the side of the car. Most of the time they would simply drive away in terror, later finding words scraped in the paint on the side of the car or even sometimes discovering a prosthetic hook hanging from the door handle.

While the story may have started as an urban myth intended to add excitement to these midnight trips to Edwin Warner Park, the tales have continued to this day. The area is no longer a lover's lane, but people who drive or walk through the park at night will sometimes report seeing a haggard man with a hook where his right hand should be.

visiting

The "Hookman" is most often encountered in the more remote corners of the park and usually at night. This makes it more than possible to find him here since the park does not officially close until 11:30 p.m. Since this does give you several hours of darkness while the park is still open, going there in your car at night and finding a secluded spot is your best bet for finding this ghost. Keep in mind, though, that you just might get your wish and hear that metallic scrape crawl along the side of your car.

FLORENCE ROAD RAILROAD CROSSING

2539 Florence Rd., Murfreesboro, TN 37129

directions

From downtown Nashville, take I-24 East to Exit 76/Medical Center Parkway. Make a right on Manson Pike, and follow this for about a mile and a half until you come across Florence Road. Turn right at Florence Road, and follow it for about a mile until you reach the railroad tracks.

history

Repeatedly, tragedy has cursed the tracks at this intersection. Perhaps the most often told account of disaster at these train tracks occurred either in the late 1970s or the early 1980s in the immediate aftermath of a nearby Halloween party. A young man from the area was desperately in love with a young woman whom he had spoken to from time to time and had seen throughout the area. Anxious to get to know her better, he invited her to a Halloween party at a tavern that sat adjacent to the railroad crossing. At the party, the man got drunk and told the woman how he felt about her. After declaring his love, he asked her to marry him. Shocked, the young woman told him that she was already married, but this didn't dissuade the man at all. He told her that she had to leave her husband and marry him, and when she refused again, he said that if she wouldn't marry him, he would jump in front of the next train and kill himself.

He made this last statement loudly, and since the alcohol was flowing rather freely at the party, everyone there decided to follow him outside to see if he would actually jump in the path of an oncoming train. The partygoers stood outside for a while, some egging him on and daring him to go through with it. His love interest begged him to go back inside, but he refused in his angry drunken haze.

Soon a train whistle erupted in the distance, and the crowd got excited. This excitement soon turned to horror, though, as the young man walked onto the train tracks. The people who had been encouraging him soon began yelling at him to get off the tracks, insisting that it wasn't funny anymore, but the young man wouldn't budge. The train wasn't able to slow down at all before it hit him. His body was never found.

While this story is the most often repeated of the calamities to occur at this section of road, many other people have met their deaths here. The intersection is considered quite dangerous because of the number of accidents that have befallen vehicles on these tracks. Many drivers will believe they can beat the train and get across the tracks before the train reaches the intersection. Many of these cars will not make it and become further statistics in the ever-growing death toll here.

Recently, a man who was walking home toward Smyrna was decapitated by a passing train near the intersection with Florence Road. Many of the victims here are buried in the Roselawn Memorial Gardens which overlooks the intersection.

ghost story

Years have passed since the party at which the young man committed suicide, but some ghostly remnants of that night seem to replay themselves every so often. Dark figures will sometimes be seen walking on or near the tracks, and ghostly train whistles and squealing train brakes will often be heard on the tracks, even when they are empty.

Most notably, however, the scene of the young man's suicide in its entirety seems to be replayed here quite often. People will sometimes see or hear a crowd gathered at the train tracks, seemingly goading someone onto the tracks or attempting to coax them away. Or people will watch a young man walk out onto the tracks directly in front of an oncoming train. This figure always vanishes as the train hits it. Occasionally, people will even encounter the ghost of the young woman, pleading with the young man to get off of the tracks. These ghosts seem to be a kind of reenactment of what happened that Halloween night in the late 1970s or early 1980s. The ghosts never interact with any of the witnesses, but rather simply replay their roles from that horrible night.

This ghost story has actually been reported by passing trains in the area. Trains will often report the suicide scene playing itself out in front of them. It will actually cause some of these trains to apply their brakes and report the incident.

visiting

This railroad crossing is readily accessible and may be visited at any time. That being said, if you do choose to visit this haunted location, be sure to exercise extreme caution. As previously mentioned, this place has been the scene of many serious accidents throughout the years. If you do visit the area, be sure to stay off the tracks. In order to encounter these ghosts, it is not imperative that you be on the tracks, just within sight of them.

Also keep in mind that this residual haunting is reported most often on Halloween night, the anniversary of the young man's suicide. If you are in the area on Halloween, that would be the best time of the year to go looking for these particular ghosts.

FORT NEGLEY

1100 Fort Negley Blvd., Nashville, TN 37203

directions

Fort Negley is just south of downtown Nashville. From Broadway, take Eighth Avenue South for a mile and a half. Turn left onto Chestnut Street. Follow Chestnut Street for less than a quarter mile. Take the second left onto Fort Negley Boulevard. The entrance to the fort will be on your right. There is a historical marker and a large flag marking the entrance.

history

When Fort Donelson fell to Union forces in 1862, the Confederates knew that there was no way they could hold Nashville. Reluctantly, the Confederates left the city, and Union forces were happy to take it over. The Union occupiers were well aware of Nashville's strategic importance, and they quickly started building fortifications around the city to defend against the counterattack that was sure to come. Fort Negley was the largest and most impressive of these forts.

Fort Negley stood atop a hill, embedded into the limestone. The fort was nearly impenetrable. When the Confederates did finally mount their counteroffensive against occupied Nashville in 1864, their forces were stopped much farther south of the city than Fort Negley. Thus Fort Negley did not see any action during the Civil War. It served more as an ominous reminder to the occupied citizens of the town that the South could not retake their city.

Fort Negley, as an enemy fort, was soon forgotten after the war and quickly became overgrown. Members of the racist group the Ku Klux Klan took advantage of the abandoned fort and began holding meetings and cross burnings within the fort. It is likely that several African Americans were lynched within the walls of this old Union fort.

ghost story

The ghostly occurrences witnessed most often within Fort Negley today are ghost lights. People driving by or walking near the area after dark will see strange balls of light floating throughout the grounds. Since the fort stands on a tall hill and is visible from all around the area, people from quite far away have seen unusual lights at Fort Negley long after the place has closed and no visitors should be inside.

Another ghost patrols the trails in and around the fort as well. People will see a Union soldier walking around within the park, and they report that he appears quite real in most aspects. Witnesses recount specifics about him including the texture of the uniform and the detail in the uniform's buttons. What makes the witnesses so certain that they have seen a ghost, though, is that the soldier has no face.

visiting

Fort Negley is accessible to the public only during the day. Unfortunately, this makes it impossible to investigate up close the ghost lights that are frequently spotted throughout the park. It is not impossible to see these ghost lights, however. Just park your car at a spot from which you can see the hill that holds the fort, and you may glimpse these ghostly lights floating through the fort.

The faceless soldier appears during the day, so you should have a much easier time accessing the park to look for him. There is a parking area near the visitor center, and admission to the grounds is free. It requires a little climb to get up to the fort, but the view is well worth it once you're there.

GALLATIN TOWN SQUARE

Public Square and North Water Street, Gallatin, TN 37066

directions

In order to get to Gallatin, take I-65 North to Exit 95, TN 386 North. Take TN 386 North toward Hendersonville/Gallatin for 17 miles, and then angle right onto Red River Road. Less than a half mile down the road, turn left onto Broadway; then take your second right onto North Water Street. Follow North Water Street to your fourth left. Turn left on Public Square, and you are in the Gallatin Town Square.

history

This area has been plagued with death and destruction almost since it was built in the late 1700s. Perhaps one of the darkest instances in the square's history occurred during the Civil War. In November of 1862, Union General Eleazar A. Paine took control of Gallatin and occupied it throughout the remainder of the war. During his brutal occupation of the town, Paine would oftentimes execute suspected spies in the town square. Many of the buildings in the square were also used as military hospitals for those wounded in nearby battles.

After the war the town square again experienced death, as an epidemic of cholera devastated Gallatin in 1873, killing upwards of 60 people in a single summer month. Many of the bodies from the epidemic were laid in the town square as the local undertakers could not handle the sudden influx of bodies.

A fire struck the town square in the early 20th century and burned a couple of the buildings to the ground. Several people were killed in the fire, and a few of the historic buildings there were completely destroyed.

Finally, in April 2006, an outbreak of tornadoes hit the town and did significant damage all around Gallatin. Nine people were killed in the tornadoes, and 150 people were seriously injured.

ghost story

Strange things seem to happen repeatedly throughout the town square. Many people relate this ghostly activity to some of the tragic events that occurred in the area.

Many apparitions are seen walking around in the town square. Most of the time, these apparitions take the form of Civil War soldiers. Witnesses will encounter men dressed in Civil War uniforms walking around the square, paying no attention to anything around them. These men will most often be seen at night and will mysteriously fade away as they are being watched.

People will also experience hot spots within the area. Even on the coldest days, people will find spots throughout the square that are quite warm. There is nothing nearby that could explain these hot spots. Perhaps they are remnants of the fire that once devastated the square.

visiting

When visiting these ghosts after dark, there are very few obstacles that stand in your way. The town square is an open, public place that can be accessed at any time during the day or night. Since most of the ghostly activity occurs at night, it is possible to roam around the square late at night, looking for the ghostly Civil War soldiers that so often are reported walking through the area.

MUSIC ROW

Music Circle East and Music Circle South,
Nashville, TN 37203

directions

Easily within walking distance from downtown, Music Row is more of a district than
an actual road. Simply take Broadway to the southwest across the bridge to 14th
Avenue South. Everything for four or five blocks in every direction from this point is
considered the Music Row area. To approach the heart of Music Row, turn left onto
14th Avenue. It will become Music Circle East at Demonbreun Street.

history

Very often, people will consider Music Row the center of the country music, Christian
music, and gospel music industries. Most of the studios that record these genres of
music are headquartered in this area. As a result, many aspiring musicians have had
their careers created or their dreams destroyed in this small geographic area just
southwest of downtown Nashville.

In the latter part of the 20th century, Music Row was a huge tourist draw for the city of Nashville. The Country Music Hall of Fame was here, as well as a slew of tourist-trap museums along Demonbreun Street. When the Opryland amusement park closed in the 1990s, the tourist trade in Nashville suffered. As a result, all of these museums shut down and were replaced by upscale restaurants.

ghost story

The dark, now rather lonely, roads of Music Row have their share of ghosts. Many suggest that the ghosts are remnants of those people whose lives and dreams were either made or broken along these streets.

Mostly, the ghost stories here involve shadowy figures that mysteriously vanish into the night. Witnesses will see, out of the corner of an eye, a dark figure walking down a road at night, but when they turn their head to look at the figure more directly, it has somehow disappeared. Some people will hear footsteps following them down the dark streets after dark but will turn around and find no one behind them.

At least one famous ghost lurks around Music Row, as well. Hank Williams Sr. (see Ryman Auditorium and Tootsie's Orchid Lounge chapters) supposedly walks here at night. People will see a man who looks exactly like Hank Williams Sr. walking down the streets. On occasion, they will actually have a conversation or in some way interact with him before he vanishes into the night. At other times, Hank will appear as a white, misty figure.

visiting

The streets of Music Row are open throughout the night, and there are places to park to explore the area. While downtown Nashville and the Music Row areas are generally good parts of town, it is probably in your best interest not to go roaming in remote areas of Music Row by yourself late at night. It may be an adventure to go looking for the ghosts here, but use a little caution and don't advertise yourself as a potential victim to someone with less than honest intentions.

PRINTERS ALLEY

Printers Alley, Nashville, TN 37201

directions

Printers Alley is the name of a haunted alley in downtown Nashville. It sits just north of Broadway and runs between and parallel to Third and Fourth avenues. It runs from Union Street to Commerce Street and is decorated with a huge neon sign which spans the road.

history

Nashville's Printers Alley got its name from its early years as the center of the city's publishing industry. Two large newspapers had their headquarters here, as well as 10 printing shops and 13 publishing companies.

By the 1940s, the publishing side of Printers Alley had waned somewhat and the area was overtaken by several nightclubs. At that time, the sale of alcohol was illegal in Nashville, but it was done openly within Printers Alley. The police purposefully looked the other way, and the mayor himself would make no secret of the fact that he was patronizing the establishments there.

By the time the alcohol ban was lifted in Nashville in 1968, Printers Alley had gained a rather seedy reputation. Nightclubs and strip joints stretched all along the short alley. Despite the rough reputation on the surface, however, it was a favorite night spot in the city and no one worked hard to shut the area down.

Perhaps the most colorful personality to ever inhabit Printers Alley was a man named Skull Schulman, who owned the Rainbow Room exotic dance club here. He had a white poodle that he often walked through the area, and he would always wear a variety of bright colors so that he resembled a rainbow himself— perhaps as a way of advertising his club. One day, Skull arrived early at his club and sat at the end of his bar, as he was accustomed. Two homeless men broke in and put a knife to his throat, demanding his money. Skull refused to give it to them. One of the assailants cut his throat with the knife. It was only a superficial wound, however, and Skull screamed loudly despite his attackers' pleas not to. Eventually one of the attackers hit him in the head with a liquor bottle, a wound that would kill him.

ghost story

Even though he died, Skull Schulman's memory and spirit continue to haunt the area. The Rainbow Room closed after Schulman's death and sat abandoned for a little while. The Bourbon Street Blues and Boogie Bar used the area for storage, but only for a short time, because the bar's employees began to refuse to go in. They said that the place was haunted. They would hear phantom sounds and would sometimes see a man with a poodle and a brightly colored sport jacket looking at them.

The ghost of Skull Schulman does not just frequent the closed Rainbow Room. He is seen all throughout the Printers Alley section of the city. Most of the time he is wearing his bright sport coat and walking a white poodle down the road. Witnesses will almost always observe him walking away from them and will not think much of it until the figure mysteriously vanishes or turns and walks through a closed door.

visiting

Despite the somewhat seedy reputation of Printers Alley, it is not necessarily a dangerous place to go. There are still night clubs that stretch down the alley, but it is not in a bad part of town by any means. There is always a chance to catch a glimpse of poor Skull Schulman if you visit the alley at any time of the day. It is definitely more exciting at night when all of the clubs are in full swing and each bar has a man outside trying to lure you in.

Your best bet for seeing the ghost here, though, is to arrive between 4 p.m. and 5 p.m. This was the time that Skull was murdered and the time he is seen most often here.

SANDERS FERRY PARK

513 Sanders Ferry Rd., Hendersonville, TN 37075

directions

When coming from downtown Nashville, take I-65 North for 12 miles to Exit 95, the Vietnam Veterans Boulevard exit toward Hendersonville/Gallatin. Follow this road for 3 miles to Exit 3, to the Johnny Cash Parkway toward Hendersonville. Follow this road for a little more than 3 miles, and then turn right onto Sanders Ferry Road. Follow Sanders Ferry Road for almost 3.5 miles, and then turn left to stay on Sanders Ferry Road. Follow the road for another mile, and it will dead-end into Sanders Ferry Park.

history

As you near the loop that encircles the park, you'll encounter a sharp turn in the road. In 1989, during a company picnic, a father got into a loud fight with his teenage son. At the climax of the argument, the teenage son got into his car in frustration and sped away from the park.

As the teenager went around the sharp turn, he disappeared behind the tree line. Those at the picnic heard his tires squealing as the car went around the turn, but they really didn't think any more of it until they heard sirens nearby. Apparently the teenager had wrecked the car while rounding the curve. He was killed in the accident.

ghost story

There are all kinds of unusual lights that appear in Sanders Ferry Park at night. People will see strange balls of light of every color floating through the park. When these balls of light are approached, they inexplicably dissipate into the darkness. Other people will see phantom headlights coming into or leaving the park that simply disappear without a trace.

A mysterious figure is also sometimes seen on the road coming into Sanders Ferry Park. The figure is a teenage boy who seems to be walking toward the park around the sharp turn in the road. Many times, this figure will just vanish as the terrified witness watches in disbelief.

visiting

The park opens at dawn and closes at 11 p.m. This leaves some time after the sun goes down to explore the park, looking for ghosts. Since many of the ghostly happenings here are lights, night is the only time that you can really experience the ghosts here. Park near one of the shelters, and simply watch the fields for the ghostly lights. On your way out, look for the teenage boy walking along the road in the dark.

SHY'S HILL

4609 Benton Smith Rd., Nashville, TN 37215

directions

Take I-65 South to Exit 78B toward TN 255 West/Harding Place. After about a half mile, the road changes its name to Battery Lane. Follow Battery Lane for another 2 miles until it changes its name again to Harding Place. Turn left onto Benton Smith Road. Shy's Hill will be on your right about 0.1 mile down the road. There is a single parking spot along the road near a trail and historic marker.

history

On the run after a crushing defeat by General William T. Sherman at Atlanta, General John Bell Hood moved his army west to try to cut off Sherman's supply lines. Sherman didn't notice, marching to the sea and living off the land on the way. Union General George H. Thomas was left to deal with Hood. Thomas took up a defensive position within Nashville itself while Hood surrounded him. On December 15, 1864, Thomas attacked Hood's army, forcing Hood to retreat somewhat as night fell.

The next day, Hood's lines stretched only about two miles, and he was quickly being flanked by Union forces. The strongest position held by Confederate forces was a hill south of Nashville that would become Shy's Hill. Union forces charged up the hill. While the Union should have been cut down by the superior strategic position of the Confederates, the hill was too steep for the Confederates to properly aim their weapons at the enemy. Union forces overwhelmed them and took the hill in a bloody skirmish. Colonel William Shy was the Confederate commander who was defending Shy's Hill. He was killed in the battle, and the hill would eventually be named for him. As a result of losing Shy's Hill, the Confederates were routed. The Army of Tennessee was essentially defunct.

Shy's Hill was littered with the dead and dying. Some bodies lay there for days before being collected and buried. Today, a small trail, a historic marker, and a cannon on the hill are three of the only remaining memorials to the fighting at Shy's Hill.

ghost story

As with many Civil War battlefields, remnants of the carnage that occurred here still echo to this day. People will hear moans and screams when they walk the trail to the top of Shy's Hill. Distant drums and cannon fire will also be detected quite often in the area. As people climb the trail to the hilltop, they will sometimes feel as if they are being followed. Sometimes they will actually hear footsteps behind them, and other times they will just experience an intangible feeling that they are being followed; but upon turning around they find that no one is there.

At night, when the trail is closed, people will still sometimes encounter things in the area. People driving by the parking area on Shy's Hill Road at the foot of the trail will see shadowy figures moving through the woods near the trailhead. Sometimes, figures dressed in Civil War uniforms will be seen walking through the area after nightfall.

visiting

You can only walk the trail that leads up to Shy's Hill from dawn to dusk. You will be trespassing if you attempt to scale the hill after nightfall. This doesn't impede ghosthunting in the area all that much, though, since many of the ghostly happenings are experienced by people during the day when they are climbing the hill. The other ghosts that tend to come out at night are often seen from Shy's Hill Road in the vicinity of the trail, so you can still look for ghosts as you drive by at night.

If you go during the day, parking is limited and larger vehicles will not fit in the area, so keep this in mind if you plan on walking the trail.

SLAUGHTER PEN AT STONES RIVER NATIONAL BATTLEFIELD

3501 Old Nashville Hwy., Murfreesboro, TN 37129

directions

Start on I-24 East and follow it for about 27 miles to Exit 74B, TN 840 East. Follow TN 840 East for about 2 miles to Exit 55A toward Murfreesboro. Follow Northwest Broad Street for a little more than 2.5 miles, and then turn right onto Thompson Lane. Take the first left onto Old Nashville Highway. When the road dead-ends, take a left onto West College Street. At the first intersection, West College Street changes its name to Old Nashville Highway. Less than a mile down the road, the visitor center for the battlefield will be on your left. Inside the park, there is a loop that travels around the battlefield. Stop 2, the Slaughter Pen, is the most haunted area of the park.

history

As the Battle of Stones River raged, Confederate forces made efforts to flank the Union on their right. In order to prevent Union forces from repositioning and circling around, the Confederates attacked the Union at their center, not in an effort to break through but to keep the Union lines in place and block their advance. General Philip Sheridan of the Union was defending a forested area near the Union center and was assaulted by Confederate forces here.

As the battle wore on, units on Sheridan's flanks collapsed, and his forces were assaulted from three sides by the enemy. Eventually, the Union forces ran low on ammunition and were forced to retreat to the north.

The losses to Union forces in the area were astronomical. Nearly all the Union units here lost a third or more of their men, and all three of Sheridan's brigade commanders were killed in the battle. The small area where this part of the battle took place was filled with the dead and wounded. For the next several days, bodies continued to be discovered in the area, some having been merely wounded during the battle but left there without medical attention. People who saw the field of battle in its aftermath remarked that it looked like a slaughter pen. The name stuck.

ghost story

Often considered the bloodiest part of the battle, the Slaughter Pen is notorious for having a lot of paranormal activity, especially during the day. Today, the area consists of a trail that goes into the woods where the fighting actually took place. People who walk the trail during the day will sometimes report hearing footsteps following the trail behind them. Despite an exhaustive search of the area, no one else is ever found.

While the footsteps are the most often reported phenomenon in the Slaughter Pen, visitors and rangers will also report hearing other things in the area. Sometimes they hear yells and screams. Sometimes they hear noises that sound like a distant battle. The Battle of Stones River still rages in this small section of woods where so many died painfully.

visiting

The great thing about the ghost story here is that it has only been reported during daylight hours when the park is open to the public. In addition, it costs nothing to visit the park and the haunted area by Stop 2 called the Slaughter Pen. Remember that the ghostly footsteps are most often reported by someone who is walking the trail alone, so you may opt to take the trail by yourself to see if you can experience the phenomenon.

TWO RIVERS GOLF COURSE

2235 Two Rivers Ct., Nashville, TN 37201

directions

Even though it is possible to get to this location using back roads from downtown, the fastest way to get here is typically to take I-40 East for about 6 miles to Exit 215B, the Briley Parkway/TN 155 North exit. Follow the parkway for about 2 miles to Exit 8; then take the Lebanon Pike exit toward Donelson. Turn right onto Lebanon Pike and continue until you reach McGavock Pike. Turn left on McGavock Pike, and follow the road three intersections past the railroad tracks to Two Rivers Parkway. The entrance to the golf course will be the first driveway after Two Rivers Parkway. If you are not there to play golf, the next driveway is the entrance to a public park that surrounds the golf course.

history

Embodying a perfect sense of tranquility, it is hard to believe that the history of the area is actually quite dark. Long before European settlers ever set foot in Tennessee, the land was frequented by Native Americans. Much of the actual land that is now used as a golf course once served as a burial ground for the Native Americans who lived here. Eventually, European settlers moved into the area, and this place's significance to the native people was forgotten.

Near the end of the Civil War, battles were waged frequently in and around all of Nashville. As thousands of men from both sides of the war died in the area, there were few cemeteries with the capacity to deal with the influx of the dead. The present site of the golf course was formerly a cemetery for many of the men who lost their lives fighting in the war.

A man once lived on the property somewhere near the back of the current golf course. He hoarded his money jealously and buried it across his property. He amassed a fortune but died before he could ever dig it up and use it for himself.

When the ground was dug to create the golf course, workers came across evidence that the area was used to bury both Native Americans and Civil War casualties. The old man's house was eventually razed, and many jars of money were discovered throughout the property.

ghost story

The golf course itself is haunted. One of the stories most often reported by both golfers and employees is sounds that suggest they are being followed. Witnesses will hear footsteps behind them or sometimes breathing, but when they turn around to see who is trailing them, nothing is there. Other times people will hear moans or pleas for help, but the source is never discovered.

Another ghostly story occurs near the back of the golf course where the old man's house once stood. People will sometimes hear the old man opening his jars of money. Perhaps the old man is finally ready to spend the fortune he hoarded all those years.

visiting

If you are a golfer and want to play a haunted course, the course is open to the public every day and costs $13 for adults to play. If you are not a golfer, you won't be able to roam the course. There is an alternative, though. The course is actually surrounded by the Two Rivers Park, and much of the ghostly activity is reported in the park as well. The site of the old man's house is near the Briley Parkway side of the course between holes 17 and 8.

TWO RIVERS PARKWAY

Two Rivers Parkway and McGavock Road,
Nashville, TN 37201

directions

Take I-40 East for about 6 miles to Exit 215B, the Briley Parkway/TN 155 North exit. Follow the parkway for about 2 miles to Exit 8; then take the Lebanon Pike exit toward Donelson. Turn right onto Lebanon Pike until you reach McGavock Pike. Turn left on McGavock Pike, and follow the road three intersections past the railroad tracks to Two Rivers Parkway. Turn left onto Two Rivers Parkway. The haunted section of road lies between McGavock Pike and the end of the Two Rivers Park.

history

Every piece of land surrounding this short road was once a cemetery (see Two Rivers Golf Course chapter). Originally, the land under and surrounding Two Rivers Parkway was used as a Native American burial ground. Later the ground became a graveyard for Civil War casualties.

A few years ago, a motorist who was driving around the curve on Two Rivers Parkway saw something strange in the brush on the side of the road. Curious, the driver stepped out of his car to investigate. To his absolute horror, he discovered the body of a young woman.

The authorities were called in to investigate, and they discovered that the young woman had been brutally murdered and her body dumped alongside the road. Despite all efforts to locate them, the killer or killers were never found.

ghost story

Very often, reports of the ghost here will all be the same. A ghostly woman will be seen walking down Two Rivers Parkway between the Two Rivers Park and McGavock Pike. Many times, those who see this woman don't think that she may be a ghost. She will look like a real person who seems somewhat dazed and confused as she stumbles down the road. Others state that it looks as if she's searching for something on the roadside.

Those who stop to ask if she needs help are met with a startling occurrence. She will suddenly look up at the person, make eye contact with him or her, and then vanish.

visiting

This is an easily accessible ghost. The road is public and therefore open throughout the night. The parkway is not a dangerous place to drive and is relatively straight. You will even find it reasonably safe to drive down the road repeatedly in the dead of night. Feel free to drive up and down the street as often as you'd like, as late as you'd like. This is your best chance to encounter this spirit.

WHITE SCREAMER OF WHITE BLUFF

White Bluff, TN 37187

directions

Take I-40 West from Nashville for about 16 miles. Take Exit 192, the McCrory Lane exit toward Pegram. Turn slightly to the right at the end of the exit onto McCrory Lane, and follow this for a little more than a mile until you reach US 70/Memphis-Bristol Highway. Turn left onto US 70. Follow this for about 13 miles, and it will take you into the heart of the haunted town of White Bluff, Tennessee.

history

Once, a man tended a farm in a hollow in White Bluff with his wife and seven children. For a while, life was happy for them, but one night loud screams began to emanate from the forest surrounding the farmland. The screams would continue for the next few nights, not only keeping the family up throughout the night but also terrifying them to the edge of reason.

The father decided that something had to be done about whatever creature was screaming out in the woods, so he took his two dogs and a shotgun out looking for the creature. At one point during the hunt, the dogs ran out in front of their owner supposedly in pursuit of the creature, but they quickly returned and ran back past the man in terror. Alone and concerned, the man followed the terrified dogs back to his homestead in the hollow. When he arrived home he found that his wife and seven children were dead, torn to shreds by some unknown force.

ghost story

Throughout White Bluff and the surrounding area, many varied stories emerge about the elusive "White Screamer." Many people in the area have heard the terrifying nighttime screams, which continue to destroy the evening silence of this small town to this day. Yet the piercing screams are the only aspect of the stories that remains uniform. Reports of people who have actually encountered the creature vary nearly every time the creature is spotted.

Some who see the creature report that it is a white, misty apparition that flits through the woods quickly and ominously in the night. These stories compare the White Screamer to the banshee of European lore, likening the screams to an omen of bad luck. Others report that the source of the screams is an actual creature that resembles an alpaca: a white furry beast that walks on all fours and stands about six feet tall with a face resembling a camel. These reports suggest that the creature does not attack humans but does kill livestock in the local fields.

Whatever the case, the White Screamer is never considered benevolent. Those from the town who know it best describe it as a creature to avoid. Some residents of White Bluff have learned to lock their doors and simply ignore the terrifying screams that provide a soundtrack for the otherwise peaceful night.

visiting

Even though encounters of the creature are relatively common, no single place in White Bluff claims more sightings of the creature than any other. The creature is rather said to haunt the community as a whole, the screams being audible throughout the small town. As a ghosthunter looking for the creature, you should probably begin looking for the creature in any wooded area of the town.

Beyond the obvious danger of actually encountering the creature, if you do enter any wooded area in the town, make sure that you stay clear of private property. Residents already on the edge from the screams that sometimes tear through the night may shoot first if they see someone or something roaming around their property.

WHITES CREEK PIKE'S DEVIL'S ELBOW

5297 Whites Creek Pike, Joelton, TN 37080

directions

North of Nashville in the small town of Joelton, Devil's Elbow is simply a dangerous curve in a road. To get there, take I-24 West for about 6 miles to Exit 43, TN 155 West. Follow TN 155 West for 2 miles to Exit 19, US 431 North/Whites Creek Pike. Merge to the right onto Whites Creek Pike, and follow the road for about 6.5 miles. The Devil's Elbow is a sharp turn to the left. The ground drops off sharply on the left side of the road, and there will be a rock wall on your right.

history

Whites Creek Pike has gained the nickname "Devil's Elbow" at a particularly sharp turn in the road that looks down into a ravine. Car accidents are quite common around this curve as many people don't realize how sharp the turn is and end up crashing into the wall or falling into the ravine. Many fatalities have resulted from the many car accidents around this turn.

On December 9, 1996, a man was grabbed by armed assailants at his nearby home. They grilled him about the whereabouts of his brother, and when they were unable to get any information from him, they shot him 12 times. They took his body to Devil's Elbow and dumped it into the ravine. The body wasn't discovered until a car fell into the ravine a month later.

ghost story

In the dead of night, people will hear what sounds like a car wrecking at the curve. Because of the frequency of accidents here, people who hear the sounds assume that they have witnessed yet another tragedy. They are usually surprised when they check the next day and find that no one wrecked there the night before. Sometimes, these witnesses actually go down to Devil's Elbow looking for the wrecked car. They find nothing there.

These ghostly crashes aren't the most famous ghost of the area, though. A faceless hitchhiker is often seen standing at the curve. There is no safe place to stop along the curve, so no one ever pulls over to pick up the hitchhiker. According to the legends, those who see the hitchhiker when they go through Devil's Elbow will have an unfortunate streak of bad luck in their lives.

visiting

Needless to say, do not stop your car in the curve at Devil's Elbow. The curve is very sharp and very blind, and you will get hit if you stop here. But it is not even necessary to stop your car in the curve in order to experience the ghost here. Since the road is public, you can drive up and down it all night long looking for the phantom hitchhiker and listening for the phantom crashes.

WICKHAM STONE PARK

Buck Smith Road and Oakridge Road, Palmyra, TN 37142

directions

Take I-65 North from downtown Nashville to Exit 86A, I-24 West. Follow I-24 for about 34 miles until Exit 11, TN 76 West. Follow TN 76 West for about 10 miles until you reach TN 13/TN 48, and turn left. About 8 miles down the road, veer to the right to stay on TN 13. Four miles down the road, turn right onto Budds Creek Road. Two miles farther, turn left onto Buck Smith Road. The collection of statues are along Buck Smith Road and Oakridge Road near their intersection about 2–3 miles down the road.

history

The sculptor, Enoch Tanner Wickham, was born in 1883 but didn't begin to build the statues that became his legacy until 1952, when he moved to his home on Buck Smith Road. The first life-size statue that he constructed was that of the Virgin Mary, but he soon started creating many others around his property. Some of the statues were of people that he knew, and others were of famous figures such as John F. Kennedy and even Babe the Big Blue Ox from the Paul Bunyan myth.

Wickham worked on little else but his sculptures for the rest of his life, and people from throughout the area would come to Palmyra in order to see these remarkable statues, which decorated a remote road in Middle Tennessee. Everyone who ever met Wickham during his life would comment on how friendly he was. When he died in 1970, his statues began to fall victim to vandalism. Many of the statues' heads have been destroyed, and many of the statues are covered with spray paint. Those who have run into Wickham since his death don't think he's as friendly as everyone said.

ghost story

The ghost stories from the area mostly involve the spirit of Wickham himself. Many people who have witnessed this ghostly activity suggest that he is protecting his statues from further vandalism. People will sometimes hear an unfamiliar male voice coming from behind them when they approach the statues, warning them to stay away. People will also report hearing a hammer hitting a chisel, perhaps the ghostly remnants of all the work Wickham put into the statues. Others will see strange shadows moving behind and between the statues, and sometimes mysterious ghostly lights will inexplicably dance throughout the area.

If the statues are closely approached or touched, the spirit seems to become a little angrier. The male voice will whisper menacingly. Occasionally, people will feel as if they've been pushed backward by some unseen force.

Another ghost story in the area suggests that a man killed his wife who was dying of pneumonia because he grew weary of caring for her. Late that night, he buried her at the base of one of Wickham's statues but was seen by his son. In a fit of rage, he killed his son as well and buried him alongside his mother. Having come to his senses, the man realized what he had done, and he killed himself in front of the same statue. Perhaps these mysterious shadows and lights have something to do with this tragedy.

visiting

Give these statues your respect as you approach them. It is unfortunate that the statues have fallen victim to vandals. It is difficult to believe that people could be so disrespectful to something so unique. People and law enforcement from the area completely agree with us, and if you approach the statues in the middle of the night, even if it is not your intent to vandalize them, you may be arrested.

This being said, it is still very possible and very easy to encounter these ghosts. The adjacent roads are open throughout the night, and you can slowly drive up and down them looking for strange shadows and listening for phantom voices. It is much safer and more respectful, though, to stay inside the car when visiting these statues at night.

For more information, see www.wickhamstonepark.com.

Wickham Stone Park, see page 183

SECTION VI

miscellaneous

ATHENAEUM RECTORY
808 Athenaeum St., Columbia, TN 38401

directions
Take I-65 South for about 31 miles to Exit 53, the Saturn Parkway exit toward Columbia/ Spring Hill. Take this road for about 4.5 miles, and then merge onto US 31 South toward Columbia. Follow this road for about 11 miles, and then turn right onto West Seventh Street. Travel this road for about a quarter mile, and then turn left onto Athenaeum Street. The Athenaeum Rectory will be the unique building on your right.

history
The Athenaeum Rectory was originally constructed as a residence for President Polk's nephew, Samuel Polk Walker, but when construction was finally completed on the building, it instead became a home for Princeton University graduate Rev. Franklin Smith.

When he moved into the house in 1837, Reverend Smith was the president of an all-girls college called the Columbia Female Institute. For a while, everything ran smoothly and the Columbia Female Institute was considered a great school for young women in the area. This all changed in 1851, when Reverend Smith was accused of having "inappropriate relations" with one of the students at the school. James Otley, the bishop of the district, forced Reverend Smith to resign in shame.

Yet forcing the resignation did not have the result Otley had intended. It seemed that everyone in the area loved Reverend Smith, and since Smith continued to profess his innocence, Bishop Otley became the one under attack from the public. Otley was forced to flee to Memphis. Smith founded another girls' school just next door to the Columbia Female Institute and called it the Columbia Athenaeum. Here, female students were actually taught the same subjects as boys of the time. The Athenaeum was in constant operation from its founding in 1851 until 1903. The rectory is the only building from the Athenaeum college that has survived.

ghost story

Within this old building, many reports of phantom footsteps have surfaced. People in the downstairs of the house will hear footsteps from upstairs, although no one is up there. When witnesses investigate these footsteps, they find nothing that could have possibly caused them.

The most famous ghost at the Athenaeum, though, is the ghost of Rev. Franklin Smith. Despite the overwhelming community support after accusations of his impropriety with a student, his reputation was left somewhat tarnished throughout the remainder of his career and life. Those who are familiar with his ghost are convinced that he is staying around trying to convince the world that he was innocent.

People outside the house will see Reverend Smith looking out the windows. Those who see him recognize him because of a portrait of him that hangs inside the building.

visiting

The most well-known ghost at the Athenaeum is not difficult to experience. There is a public road that runs alongside the building, so anyone can park a car there and look up at the building for the apparition in the window. It is probably best to do this during the day, not because of any legal or safety issues, but because the windows in the house are next to impossible to see into at night.

In order to enter the house to listen for the phantom footsteps, you would have to go during a tour during regular business hours. The Athenaeum is open Tuesday through Saturday, 10 a.m. to 4 p.m.; from 1 p.m. Sunday. Admission is $5 for adults.

AUSTIN PEAY STATE UNIVERSITY

601 College St., Clarksville, TN 37044

directions

Take I-24 West from downtown Nashville for about 38 miles until you get to Exit 11, Martin Luther King Parkway. Take Martin Luther King Parkway toward Clarksville for a little more than 3.5 miles, and then turn right onto US 41A/Madison Street. Follow Madison Street for about 5 miles, and then turn right onto University Avenue. In less than a half mile, turn right onto College Street. The university will be on your left.

history

Officially, the college itself was founded in 1927, but the history of many of the academic buildings on the campus goes back quite a bit farther. Some of these buildings were used as learning facilities as early as the 1830s. The college itself gets its name from a former governor of Tennessee. Austin Peay died the year that the college was founded while he was still in office. To this day, Austin Peay is the only governor of Tennessee to have ever died while in office.

A story comes from the Trahern Theater that a young woman named Margaret was somehow jilted by her lover, and as a result, she entered the theater and hung herself there.

ghost story

Several ghosts roam this campus. In Browning Hall, Elizabeth Hall, and the English department, students and faculty will often report footsteps and doors opening and closing by themselves. Others will report objects that were placed in one spot the night before having been moved to a different spot the next day.

Two popular ghosts reside here at Austin Peay State University. The first of these is supposedly the ghost of Austin Peay himself. Since much of his governorship was spent trying to better the educational system of Tennessee, he is often seen roaming the campus, admiring the university, and supposedly checking on things. Students and faculty who encounter him will recognize him from photos that they've seen around the campus.

The other ghost, which haunts the Trahern Theater, is reputed to be the ghost of Margaret. Lockers and doors will often slam shut for no reason and then will open and close again. The figure of a young woman will sometimes be observed in the elevator but will disappear before reaching the elevator's next stop. If someone is in the theater's auditorium late at night, he or she will sometimes hear a young woman's voice clearly say the trespasser's name.

visiting

Only students and faculty can actually enter the structures on campus. They are the only ones who have access to the buildings where the ghostly activity is said to occur most often. If you're not a student, though, you can still wander the grounds of the campus, trying to find Austin Peay as he roams. You could also access the theater if the college is putting on some kind of production there. The schedule of events at the Trahern varies, however, so you would have to visit the university's website or view the schedule of events at the theater itself to find out when the theater is accessible to the public.

BELL WITCH CAVE

430 Keysburg Rd., Adams, TN 37010

directions

Out in the distant Nashville suburb of Adams, to get here take I-24 West from downtown toward Clarksville. Take Exit 19, TN 256 toward Adams, and follow this road for about 8 miles. Turn left onto Cedar Hill Road. After another 2.5 miles, turn right onto South Church Street/TN. Another half mile down this road, turn right onto US 41. Then turn left on Keysburg Road. The Bell Witch Cave is on your right.

history

In 1804, John Bell moved to the property along the Red River where the Bell Witch Cave is located today. He became a deacon in the local church, and he and his family grew quite prosperous. One of his neighbors, Kate Batts, felt that he had cheated her out of some of her land and was never shy about saying so. About the time that the Bells' daughter Betsy started seeing a local boy named Joshua Gardner, neighbor Kate died, and John Bell finally felt that he had nothing to worry about from the crazy woman who lived next door.

He was wrong.

ghost story

In 1817, the Bell family started to experience many weird things. First, strange, demonic-looking creatures would often be seen on the farm. Eventually, the family would hear knocking sounds coming from outside the house that would keep everyone up throughout the night. Soon the knocking sounds moved inside the house. Then the Bells would hear other phantom noises like chains being dragged across the floor, breathing, and gulping sounds.

These unexplained happenings continued to terrify the Bell family. They told friends, and others started experiencing mysterious sounds and occurrences, too. Soon, the ghost began to talk. People would ask the ghost what it was. Sometimes it would claim to be some sort of demon. Other times, it would claim to be the result of a witch's curse. Once it said that its name was Kate. From then on, it was known as Kate Batts or the "Bell Witch."

When asked why it was haunting the house, the ghost replied that it had two goals. One was to break up the relationship between Betsy and Joshua. The other was to kill John Bell. Betsy got the worst of the physical abuse from the witch. Her hair was pulled. She was attacked and scratched mercilessly. John Bell began to feel a lot of emotional and psychological strain from the haunting. He fell ill and died, leading some to believe that the ghost had killed him. The ghost's constant torment of Betsy caused her to break up with her beau, Joshua. Its goals accomplished, the Bell Witch said that she would return to the property in seven years.

As promised, seven years later the hauntings began again, only this time without such dire results. The ghost stated that it would return again in 107 years, in 1935. By 1935, the Bells' farmhouse had been torn down since so many curious paranormal enthusiasts would come to explore the property. Despite the lack of a house to haunt, the ghost returned in 1935, attacking people and speaking to them. Most of the hauntings then centered around a small cave that was on the Bells' property.

Many say that the hauntings still haven't stopped.

visiting

Even if you don't plan on entering the cave itself, you still need to pay admission to simply approach the cave. The cave itself has been added to the National Register of Historic Places, so tours of the cave and the property are constantly offered. The tours run daily from 10 a.m. until 5 p.m., with the final tour starting at around 4:15 p.m. These tours cost $11 per person with a minimum of two people required to start a tour. It is also possible to reserve a special tour of the cave. These tours are $25 per person and include a candlelight visit to an adjacent cabin and an hour-long tour of the cave. There are other special tours available as well, which focus more on the ghosts themselves.

CUMBERLAND UNIVERSITY

1 Cumberland Sq., Lebanon, TN 37087

directions

Take I-40 East for about 30 miles to Exit 238, US 231 South. At the end of the exit ramp, turn left onto US 231 and follow this road for a little more than a mile and a half. Turn left onto West Spring Street, and then turn left onto Cumberland Square. This brings you into the campus. The three buildings that are reputedly haunted are the Doris and Harry Vise Library, the Mary White Dormitory, and Memorial Hall.

history

News came during one Christmas break at the Mary White Dormitory, a women's dorm, that a murderer had escaped from a prison near Lebanon. The dorm was mostly empty, but those students who were still there were told to keep their doors locked. Two roommates remained in the building, and late one night, one of them had to go out to use the restroom. They devised a secret knock so that one roommate could keep the room's door locked while the other visited the restroom, and the one staying behind would know it was her roommate when she returned. About a half hour after the student left for the restroom, a frantic knock sounded at the door. Not hearing the code knock, the woman didn't open the door, instead staying as quiet as possible. Several hours later, she left the room, finding, to her horror, her roommate brutally murdered in the blood-covered hallway.

At Memorial Hall, a young man was waiting for his class to begin on the third floor. He was sitting on a windowsill inside the classroom and leaning back against the window. Unexpectedly, the window popped out and the young man fell to his death. Another incident at Memorial Hall involved a science teacher who had a heart attack and died after descending the stairs from the third floor.

The Vise Library has little history and even less dark history. The building was built in 1987 and has been nothing more than a library since then.

ghost story

In the Mary White Dormitory, a large variety of paranormal incidents seem to happen quite often. Televisions in the dorm rooms will turn on and off by themselves. The televisions generally turn on when both roommates are out of the room and the door is locked. Open doors will suddenly and violently slam closed. The showers in the bathrooms will turn on by themselves as well. When dorm rooms are locked and both roommates are gone, the residents will return to find that the locked room has somehow been ransacked. Items will have been thrown all over the place and posters torn down from the walls. Refrigerator doors will mysteriously open during the night.

At Memorial Hall, doors on the third floor will open and slam closed when no one is near them. People will feel an unseen presence push past them on the stairs of the building. Perhaps this is the ghost of the science professor who died of a heart attack after descending these stairs.

At the Vise Library, two ghosts are often seen. The first is a ghost cat. A gray blur, about the size and shape of a cat, will seem to float across the floor and then disappear behind something. Those who see the cat never notice the legs or paws, merely seeing a misty shape that looks like a cat float across the floor. A little girl also haunts the library, ducking behind shelves in some kind of eternal game of peek-a-boo.

visiting

Finding these ghosts can end up becoming quite difficult if you are not a student at the university. Unfortunately, you may only visit the Mary White Dormitory if you are a student and reside there. Memorial Hall is almost equally inaccessible to those who are not Cumberland students. However, the Vise Library is accessible to the public. It is open until 10 p.m. every day of the week except Friday, when it is open until 4:30 p.m., and Saturday, when it remains closed. Pick up a book, relax, and maybe see a ghost cat float by at your feet.

DOWNTOWN PRESBYTERIAN CHURCH

154 Fifth Ave. N., Nashville, TN 37219

directions

In the heart of downtown Nashville, just off Broadway, sits the Downtown Presbyterian Church. If you're going up Broadway from the river, turn right onto Fifth Avenue. The church is a little more than a block up Fifth Avenue on the corner of Church Street and Fifth Avenue. The front entrance to the church has two large white pillars and a small black metal fence at the street.

history

Historically, there are many reasons that this church may be haunted. The first worshippers at this particular church used a building at the same site as early as 1816. This building burned to the ground in a large fire in 1832. The new church that was built on the site survived only 16 years, burning down in another fire in 1848. That same year, William Strickland (see Tennessee State Capitol chapter) designed the new church using many elements from Egyptian architecture, which was popular at the time. This is one of three remaining churches in the country built to resemble an Egyptian tomb.

After the battle of New Orleans, Andrew Jackson accepted a ceremonial sword on the steps of the church. James K. Polk was inaugurated governor of Tennessee on the site. When the Civil War broke out and Nashville became occupied by the Federals, Union forces used the church as a hospital. Dubbed Nashville's Union Hospital Number 8, the building held 206 hospital beds and saw a lot of wounded and dying men.

When floods hit Nashville in the 1920s, refugees from the city were given shelter within the church.

ghost story

Even though there is only one ghost story that is reported inside this large structure, this ghost is actually seen quite often. People will often see shadow figures roaming throughout the building. Witnesses will report seeing a dark, shadowy figure out of the corner of an eye that completely vanishes when they turn to look at it. Sometimes, people actually investigate these figures, since the witnesses are so certain they saw someone. Yet no matter how much searching they do, they cannot find anyone in the vicinity.

visiting

One of the more remarkable aspects of these ghosts is the frequency of the sightings. People will observe these shadowy figures quite often inside the church. The church is, of course, open for services on Sunday mornings, but your best chance of encountering these phantom figures is during the week. The church is open from 9 a.m. to 3 p.m. on weekdays, offering Nashvillians an opportunity to stop in during a break from work to worship or just to find some quiet time. If you are quiet and respectful when you enter, you increase your chances of seeing these apparitions.

ELLIS MIDDLE SCHOOL

100 Indian Lake Rd., Hendersonville, TN 37075

directions

Take I-65 North for about 11 miles to Exit 95, the Vietnam Veterans Boulevard. Follow the Vietnam Veterans Boulevard for 3 miles to Exit 3, Johnny Cash Parkway/Gallatin Road/West Main Street. Take this road toward Hendersonville for 4 miles. Turn right onto Indian Lake Road. The middle school will be just past a large field on your right. It is instantly recognizable by the large dome in the center of the building.

history

This site was vacant until a man named Colonel Barry moved onto the property. Colonel Barry had a house and farmland that stretched throughout the area between Main Street and Indian Lake Road. Eventually Colonel Barry passed away, and the land was purchased by Hendersonville to create a school.

The school was originally a high school, but the high school was later moved elsewhere and the high school building became the middle school.

ghost story

Rumors circulate throughout the school that Colonel Barry haunts the building. Much of the time, the experiences with Colonel Barry amount to nothing more than footsteps. Students, faculty, and custodial staff will all hear footsteps coming toward them and then look up to see an empty hallway or room. People occasionally hear doors open and close throughout the building but will see no one when they investigate the sounds. The opening and closing of doors happens most frequently in the girls' restroom near the seventh-grade hall.

People also report actually seeing an apparition of the colonel. Most of the time, Colonel Barry will appear somewhere on the second floor of the building. He has been seen at the railing on the upper level of the gym and in the windows of the library on the second floor. He is always dressed in period clothing and never interacts with anyone who sees him.

visiting

Entering the building to look for ghosts is not feasible for an outsider since this building is an operational middle school. This means that you are most likely to run into the colonel if you actually attend the school or somehow gain employment here. In most cases, of course, these two approaches would be impossible. If you don't attend the school and can't get a job here, your best bet is to watch the second-floor windows at night. Maybe you'll catch a glimpse of the colonel.

FOURTH AVENUE PARKING AREA/ALLEY

120 Fourth Ave. S., Nashville, TN 37203

directions

In the heart of Nashville, hidden behind several businesses on Fourth Avenue, this parking lot apparently has several of its own ghosts. Just take Broadway from the river to Fourth Avenue, and turn left. The lot is a large one on the left side of the road that stretches from Broadway on one side to Third Avenue by Past Perfect on the other side. It is across the street from the Hilton Nashville Downtown.

history

While the site of this parking lot has a very long history, having been in the center of Nashville since the city was founded in the 1700s and near the place where many bodies and wounded were moved during the Civil War, the ghostly history may have its origins in an incident that happened here in 1997.

On a Sunday afternoon in 1997, a couple, co-owners of a nearby restaurant, were walking into the parking lot to their car when they were approached by two armed assailants. One of the assailants, just 15 years old, shot both the man and the woman. The woman died in the parking lot. The husband was rushed to the hospital and survived.

ghost story

Ghosts supposedly roam this parking area and alley in the heart of downtown. The presence of ghosts here seems odd at first since there is so much hustle and bustle in the immediate area, but nonetheless multiple reports have circulated of strange things happening throughout this parking lot.

The most common accounts are of phantom sounds in the lot. People will hear screams or crying, but when they look for the source of the sounds, nothing is there. On occasion, people will hear car doors closing or footsteps behind them but when they investigate, they find no one else in the lot.

Witnesses will also see dark, shadowy figures in the parking lot. These figures will only be seen for an instant before they disappear behind a car or around a corner. When the witnesses approach these figures, they find that no one is there.

Even when nothing tangible is present, people will often experience feelings of discomfort. It almost seems as if some spirit is here in the parking lot that just wants to be alone.

visiting

It is entirely possible to walk through this parking lot at any time of the day or night. The best time to go looking for ghosts is late at night after the excitement of Nashville's night life has died down and the parking lot is mostly empty. Make sure that if you walk through the parking lot at this time, you stay safe. Don't walk here alone late at night, and stay clear of any people that look as if they may be up to no good.

GRAND OLE OPRY HOUSE

2802 Opryland Dr., Nashville, TN 37214

directions

When coming from downtown, take Seventh Avenue North until you get to Charlotte Avenue. Turn left onto Charlotte Avenue, and it will soon become James Robertson Parkway. Take the ramp onto US 31 East North/Ellington Parkway, and follow this road for about 5 miles until the TN 155 East/Briley Parkway exit. Follow TN 155 East toward Opryland until you reach Exit 12, McGavock Pike West. Merge onto Music Valley Drive. You will take your first right and then your first left to bring you into the Opryland Plaza area. The Grand Ole Opry House is behind the gigantic Gaylord Opryland Resort.

history

Greatly popular today, the Grand Ole Opry radio show started in 1925 as an hour show that played every Saturday night. It began to increase in popularity quickly and made country music a nationwide phenomenon. To this day, no one would dispute that the greatest stage in all of country music is the Grand Ole Opry.

The Grand Ole Opry has had many homes throughout its long life, including the Ryman Auditorium in downtown Nashville (see Ryman Auditorium chapter).

However, since 1974 (with short hiatuses during the winter, when it moves to the Ryman, and with a break due to flood damage in 2010), the home of the Grand Ole Opry has been the Grand Ole Opry House in the Opryland Plaza.

The Grand Ole Opry is the reason that Nashville has become the center of the country music world, and all of the greatest country music stars have at one time or another played on this stage. During the opening performance in 1974, President Richard Nixon attended and actually played piano on stage.

No deaths have occurred within the building itself. The building has been overflowing with emotion, though, since its construction. Country music stars can finally confirm they have made it when they walk onto this stage. The closest to death anyone has come within the building was when a stagehand fell victim to a heart attack while in the building. He later died at the hospital but suffered the attack while inside the Grand Ole Opry.

ghost story

Despite the incredible amount of emotion that has played out on this stage, there are remarkably few ghost stories about the building. The ghost story that is repeated most often suggests that the ghosts here never want the performing to end—they want the show to continue indefinitely.

Stagehands and employees who are closing down the house after a night's performances will draw the curtains and kill the lights before leaving. This is a ritual they never forget to do. Despite having turned off the lights and closed the curtains, as the employees are leaving, they turn back toward the stage and see that the lights are on and the curtain has mysteriously opened.

visiting

This is a very difficult ghost to encounter firsthand. First of all, the management at the site will not discuss ghosts or hauntings with anyone despite the superstition that it is good luck to run a haunted theater. Second and probably most important, the time when the ghosts come out at the theater is after all of the patrons have left and the employees are closing down for the night.

It is well worth your time to attend a show at the Grand Ole Opry, as this represents a slice of country music history and a central piece in the history of Nashville itself. It may be difficult, though, to find a ghost while you're here, despite the fact that the building is haunted.

HUME-FOGG HIGH SCHOOL

700 Broadway, Nashville, TN 37203

directions

The Hume-Fogg High School is a large school in the heart of downtown Nashville on Broadway. Just take Broadway to the west away from the river for about seven blocks. The school takes up the entire block between Seventh and Eighth avenues and will be on the right-hand side of the road. It looks a lot like a castle.

history

In 1855, Hume School on Eighth Avenue and Broadway became the first public school in the entire city of Nashville. No other public school existed until the Fogg School opened in 1875 on the same block as Hume. By 1912, the schools had combined into the single school that remains in operation today. The impressive building stands five stories tall and also includes a basement and several entrances to the tunnel system that runs underneath the city of Nashville.

In the 1920s, a suicide occurred in the building. Feeling distraught over something, a young girl leapt from the balcony in the auditorium. There are also stories about another suicide earlier in the building's history. Legend says that one of the building's principal architects was worried over funding difficulties during the building's construction. He jumped to his death from a fourth-floor window that faced Broadway.

In the 1930s, two boys were horsing around by the swimming pool when somehow they both fell into the pool. They became entangled with one another and were unable to swim to the top. Their soaked clothing dragged them to the bottom of the pool, and both boys ended up drowning.

ghost story

Hume-Fogg seems to be infested with ghosts. People will feel as if they are being watched or glimpse a shadowy presence out of the corner of an eye. The tunnels that run underneath the school are apparently infested with shadow people and strange sounds. In October of every year, the tunnels are actually opened up for a ghost tour that travels through them. The most commonly reported ghosts are not in the tunnels, however, but instead in other sections of the school.

Sometimes, a window on the fourth floor, facing Broadway, opens by itself in the middle of the night. Perhaps this is a replay of the suicidal architect opening the window for the last time before his fateful leap.

Other ghostly activity occurs in the old swimming pool room in the school's basement. The light in the pool room will come on by itself. What makes this phenomenon even stranger is that sometimes when the lights in the swimming pool room turn on by themselves, people can see the lights' reflection in the water of the pool. And yet, since the pool has not been used for some time, it contains no water.

And so there is nothing that the lights should be reflecting off of. When this light phenomenon occurs, sometimes you can also hear faint cries for help.

visiting

Unfortunately, since this is an operating high school, it is off-limits to the public. You cannot just walk in off the street to tour the impressive building. It is still not impossible to experience the ghosts here, however. The window that opens on the fourth floor can be seen from Broadway. If you walk by the enormous structure at night, make sure you glance up at the fourth floor to look for windows that might be ajar.

The school also offers a ghost tour of the haunted tunnels every October. This is well worth checking into, because it is the only time during the year that the tunnel system is open to anyone.

NASHVILLE PUBLIC LIBRARY

615 Church St., Nashville, TN 37219

directions

The Nashville Public Library lies in the heart of downtown Nashville, just a block north of Broadway. It sits between Church Street and Commerce Street and between Sixth and Seventh avenues.

history

Encompassing an entire city block in downtown Nashville, the Nashville Public Library's main branch is huge, with three floors of books, computers, movies, and music. Before the library was built in 2001, the area held a downtown shopping mall. The library was built within the shell of the mall.

Soon after the library opened, a homeless man would frequent a corner of the library. In order to avoid the harsh cold of the street, he would retreat to this warm corner of the library and lay his head down on a table to rest. One day, closing time came around and the homeless man wasn't leaving. When the library staff approached him, they discovered that he was dead.

ghost story

Strange things will happen all throughout this building. There is a ghost that haunts the corner where the homeless man was found dead. Witnesses will see a shadowy figure sitting with his head down on the table. Often this figure is seen out of the corner of a witness's eye, and then when the witness turns to look at the figure, the table is empty.

Yet this isn't the only shadow figure seen in the building. All throughout the library, people will glimpse dark, shadowy figures and then turn to find no one actually there. Witnesses will pass an aisle of books and notice someone, but when they turn down the aisle, they find no one there.

The books in the library seem to move around in strange ways. Books are found in sections where they don't belong. While this can be explained away as perhaps the work of an innocent browser reshelving the books in the wrong place, often the locations of these books are unusual. Sometimes the books are found on the tops of shelves or in other unreachable places. No one can provide any explanation as to how they got there.

visiting

To experience the ghosts here, you would need to enter the library while it is open. The library is closed on Monday, but is open from 9 a.m. to 6 p.m. Tuesday through Friday, 9 a.m. to 5 p.m. on Saturday, and 2 p.m. to 5 p.m. on Sunday. The library has its own garage that allows visitors to park there for up to 90 minutes at no charge.

Ghostly activity has been experienced all throughout the library, so there is not a specific place that you are especially likely to see a ghost. Just browse through the large library, and you may happen to encounter something paranormal.

OLD TENNESSEE STATE PRISON

6410 Centennial Blvd., Nashville, TN 37209

directions

Start by taking I-40 West for about 4 miles to Exit 204A, Briley Parkway/TN 155 North. Follow Briley Parkway for a little more than 2 miles, and then exit at East Centennial Boulevard, Exit 26A. Less than a quarter mile from the exit off of the expressway, turn left onto a small road called Bomer Boulevard. The Old Tennessee State Prison will be the imposing structure at the end of this road.

history

This structure opened its doors and started admitting prisoners on February 12, 1898. It was constructed to resemble an imposing fortress that would instill fear and hopelessness into the newly arriving inmates. When it was first built, it contained only 800 cells. Since there were more than 1,400 prisoners that arrived at the new prison, it was immediately overcrowded. There was no ventilation in the building, so the atmosphere was constantly stuffy and uncomfortable. Numerous sanitary issues also led to illness throughout the prison.

As a result of these terrible prison conditions, many escape attempts and riots occurred during the years the prison was in operation. In 1905, several African American inmates took control of the segregated "white wing" and held hostages for several hours. In 1907, a few inmates drove a vehicle through the main gate of the prison in an escape attempt. In 1938, a large number of prisoners staged a mass escape. The effort failed, and several inmates were killed. Two other deadly riots occurred here in 1975 and 1985.

A number of fires broke out at the prison throughout the years as well. One of the fires was deadly. The mess hall caught fire, killing several trapped inmates.

By 1989, overcrowding and other concerns raised the need for another facility to be built, and in 1992 the Old Tennessee State Prison closed its doors forever.

ghost story

Nowhere are ghosts more likely to manifest themselves than in an abandoned prison.

People will often hear cell doors opening and slamming throughout the prison. When these sounds are investigated, there is no sign of any doors that have moved and no sign of anyone who may have been opening and closing them. Witnesses will occasionally encounter apparitions throughout the building. Men dressed in inmate clothing will be seen walking the many corridors, and they will mysteriously vanish when approached. Also, footsteps are heard throughout the prison almost constantly. Curious witnesses and guards will search for the source of these footsteps but are never able to find them.

Other apparitions are seen by witnesses who are outside of the building. Ghosts walk around the exercise yards, and they often look out from the prison's windows. Sometimes, passersby will hear the sound of clanging metal coming from inside, even when the building is supposedly empty.

visiting

In the 1990s, tours of the building were offered to curious people who wanted to see how inmates lived here. More recently, though, safety concerns have forced the administration to close the building to tourists. The former prison is old and uncared for, and it is now incredibly dangerous for anyone to enter the structure.

At times, you are still able to approach the building, however. Sometimes, the guards just outside the gates will allow you to approach as long as you stay in your vehicle. Your best chance of seeing or hearing a ghost would be to drive up and watch and listen. If there are no guards in the guard house, you shouldn't drive up to the prison. "No Trespassing" signs are clearly posted all along the roadway.

PALACE THEATER

146 N. Water Ave., Gallatin, TN 37066

directions

Take I-65 North to Exit 95, TN 386 North. Take TN 386 North toward Hendersonville/ Gallatin for 17 miles, and then angle right onto Red River Road. Less than a half mile down the road, turn left onto Broadway; then take your second right onto North Water Avenue. The Palace Theater will be on your right.

history

Entering the scene in 1913 and still in operation to this day, the Palace Theater is one of the oldest movie theaters not only in the state of Tennessee but in the United States. In its early days, the theater regularly showed silent movies and was a major social center in Gallatin throughout the first part of the 20th century.

For 64 years, the Palace operated as a neighborhood cinema for the town of Gallatin. In 1977, with the advent of the multiplex and the fall of the neighborhood theater, the Palace closed its doors and became little more than an abandoned storefront on Water Avenue.

When the Palace's longtime owner, Bill Roth, passed away in 1990, the property was auctioned off. It was discovered that the theater was the oldest movie theater still standing in Tennessee. Greater Gallatin Inc. had the theater named a national historic landmark and went about renovating the building. In 1994, the theater reopened for business and still shows movies every weekend. At other times, the theater serves as a venue for live performances and lectures.

ghost story

When renovations on the Palace Theater started in 1994, strange things began to happen there. According to many paranormal experts, renovations to any historic building tend to kick up a lot of ghostly activity, and the Palace is apparently no exception to this theory. Many who experienced these ghosts then and now claim that the spirit is that of William Roth, who owned and operated the theater during its original 64 years of business.

Most of the stories here involve people feeling a presence with them in the building. They will feel as if they are being watched or followed when walking alone through the theater, but when they look around no one is there. People will occasionally see figures, especially in the lobby or the projection booth, which mysteriously disappear before their eyes, or they will hear footsteps walking through the lobby when no other person is present.

visiting

The theater is still in operation as a movie cinema on the weekends, with shows usually on Friday night and Sunday afternoon. These would be the easiest times to gain access to the building in order to search for the ghosts. The Palace hosts shows and lectures at other times, but the schedule for these fluctuates depending upon the events. The only feasible time to enter the building to look for its resident spirits is during one of the film showings or other special events.

ROCK CASTLE

139 Rock Castle Ln., Hendersonville, TN 37075

directions

You can get to Rock Castle by taking I-65 North to Vietnam Veterans Boulevard, Exit 95 toward Hendersonville and Gallatin. Follow this road for 3 miles to Exit 3, the Johnny Cash Parkway. Follow the Johnny Cash Parkway toward Hendersonville for 4 miles, and then turn right onto Indian Lake Road. Follow Indian Lake Road for 2 miles. Indian Lake Road will turn sharply to the left, but keep going straight onto Rock Castle Lane. The Rock Castle will be on your right.

history

The Rock Castle home is one of the oldest structures in all of Tennessee. It was built in 1783 and is the oldest stone home in Middle Tennessee. Daniel Smith built the structure under the supervision of his wife Sarah. Since Daniel was an important surveyor and a captain during the American Revolution, he was away from home much of the time. His wife was forced to take over the 3,140-acre plantation and supervise construction of the house. Much of the design elements can be attributed to her.

In the late 1700s, numerous Native American attacks continued in the area, and the Rock Castle Plantation was the site of several skirmishes in which both Native Americans and settlers were killed. Eventually, the plantation would be a successful business endeavor with a team of slaves and employees, many of whom are buried in the cemeteries on the property.

Today, the house and 18 surrounding acres constitute a museum, which is run by the Tennessee Historical Commission and is open to the public.

ghost story

Visible spirits seem to live within the walls and around the grounds of this historic building. Witnesses will sometimes see people in period dress walking around inside the building. When they go to investigate these figures, the witnesses can find no trace of them anywhere. Much more commonly, people outside the building will either see or photograph ghostly figures inside, even when the building is empty. These figures will be staring out of the windows at the witnesses and will then slowly dissipate into the darkness within.

Several strange light phenomena occur on the grounds of the Rock Castle. People will see balls of light suddenly appear throughout the grounds after dark. These lights will most often show up in the area around the cemeteries on the property. In addition, sometimes the motion-sensor lights that overlook the graveyards will suddenly come on even when no one is near them.

visiting

Unfortunately, during most of the year, the Rock Castle grounds close at dark. During every month except January and February, when the museum is closed entirely, the house and grounds are open for tours from 9 a.m. to 5 p.m., and this is your best and only opportunity to find the ghosts here.

After dark, the grounds are closed and are not visible from the public road. The only way to see the ghostly lights in the cemetery at night is when the Rock Castle holds its ghost tours and Halloween events in October. During these events, you can enter the property at night and experience the strange lights by the cemeteries.

RYMAN AUDITORIUM

116 Fifth Ave. N., Nashville, TN 37219

directions

The Ryman is located in the heart of downtown Nashville. The historic front of the auditorium is located on Fifth Avenue just off of Broadway, while the new entrance and box office are located on Fourth Avenue.

history

No one questions the unofficial title of the Ryman Auditorium as "Mother Church of Country Music," but few know that the building was actually used as a church when it was first built. Captain Thomas G. Ryman built the Ryman Auditorium for Reverend Samuel Jones's congregation in 1890. In 1897, the Tennessee Centennial Exposition came to Nashville, and a balcony was added to the auditorium to honor the Confederate soldiers who fought in the Civil War. It was originally named the Union Gospel Tabernacle, and it continued to be a church until 1906, when Reverend Jones passed away. At that time, it was already named the Ryman Auditorium after Captain Ryman, who had died two years earlier.

Eventually, the building was used almost exclusively as a venue for musical acts and became a central structure in the burgeoning musical phenomenon known as country music. For a time, this was the place that The Grand Ole Opry was recorded. Country music legends such as Roy Acuff, Minnie Pearl, Patsy Cline, Johnny Cash, Loretta Lynn, and Hank Williams Sr. all played here at the Ryman. It was declared a National Historic Landmark in 2001.

ghost story

Stories hold that at least three ghosts exist within the auditorium's walls. The first ghost is supposedly that of Captain Thomas Ryman himself. Since Ryman wanted the

building to be used primarily for religious purposes, his spirit became upset when the building became an entertainment venue. During many concerts at the Ryman, the ghost of Captain Ryman will often make his presence known when any performances do not meet his approval. During an excessively tawdry show in the early 1900s, the ghost made an appearance, creating so much noise and commotion that those watching the show were unable to hear the performers.

Another ghost that often appears in the Ryman is well known among the employees and performers and has been dubbed the "Gray Man." Musicians and staff will see the Gray Man most often during rehearsals. He will be sitting in the balcony area. They describe him as a rather nondescript man who is always dressed in gray clothing. When the balcony is searched, no trace of a man dressed in gray is ever found.

The most famous ghost of the Ryman Auditorium, though, is that of Hank Williams Sr. Many theatergoers and employees have reported seeing the music legend all throughout the building. He is always described as being a white, misty figure that will mysteriously vanish when approached. Sometimes people will run into the ghost backstage, while others will see the figure singing on stage. The ghost of Hank Williams Sr. is also reported in Tootsie's Orchid Lounge next door (see Tootsie's Orchid Lounge chapter).

visiting

Even though the Ryman is an active performance hall with regular shows and concerts, it is still possible to tour the building from 9 a.m. to 4 p.m. (It is closed Thanksgiving, Christmas Day, and New Year's Day.) While the standard tour is available every day, the backstage tour, which you can take for a slight additional charge, is subject to the concert and event schedule.

You may visit the ghosts here either by paying to see a performance, or by simply showing up earlier in the day to take a tour of the building. Since Hank Williams Sr. is often seen in the backstage area, it may be worth the extra money to take the extended backstage tour.

ST. MARY'S CATHOLIC CHURCH

460 Fifth Ave. N., Nashville, TN 37219

directions

Near both the State Capitol building and the Tennessee State Museum, this beautiful Catholic church lies in the heart of downtown Nashville on Fifth Avenue North between Charlotte Avenue and Gay Street. It sits at the foot of Capitol Hill and in the midst of many of Nashville's most recognizable landmarks.

history

This historic church was built in 1847 and was, for many years, the center of the city's Catholic community. When constructed, it was one of the largest structures in the entire state, and it continues to be a beautiful architectural landmark today.

During construction of the church, a priest decided to visit the site in order to view the progress. Unfortunately, as he was inside the church, a piece of stone fell from several stories up and struck the priest in the head. He was killed instantly.

Nashville's first bishop, Richard Pius Miles, died in 1860 and was buried in a crypt in the basement of the church. The crypt was lost to history until 1969, when it was rediscovered.

During the Civil War, a chaplain in the Confederate army was shot during a nearby battle. In an attempt to save him, he was rushed to St. Mary's, but his wounds were too severe and he died within the church's walls.

ghost story

It is no wonder that ghosts are said to walk here since this building has played such a long and important role in the history of the city. Most of the ghostly activity here is visual. People will see figures dressed as priests walking through the building at all times of the day. When these figures are questioned or approached, they will simply vanish. Many times the clothing of these priests looks like it is from the mid-1800s or from around the time of the Civil War.

Beyond the visual apparitions, though, sometimes unexplainable sounds are heard throughout the building. Footsteps will echo even when there is no one walking. People will hear loud knocking on doors and upon further investigation find no one present. One night, a monsignor who lived at the church was awakened by a knocking at his door. When he chose to ignore this sound, the knocking moved to his headboard.

People suggest that the ghosts here are either that of the priest who was killed during construction, the ghost of the chaplain killed during the Civil War, or the ghost of Bishop Miles. The theory that one ghost belongs to Bishop Miles is supported by the fact that after his crypt was rediscovered in 1969, reports of paranormal activity here reduced dramatically. Perhaps the bishop has finally found rest.

visiting

Unfortunately, this location is very difficult to visit with the intention of searching for ghosts. The church is only open to the public during the hour immediately preceding Mass and then during Mass. In the hour before Mass, you can go inside and take photographs of the historic building, but since this is still a house of worship, active ghosthunting while people are gathering for Mass would be somewhat offensive and should be avoided. It is well worth attending Mass in the historic church for the experience alone, but it is impossible to gain access to the building solely to search for ghosts. Perhaps the ghosts like it this way, having the ability to forever walk the building in peace.

SUNTRUST MORTGAGE SERVICES

201 Fourth Ave. N., Nashville, TN 37219

directions

The SunTrust Mortgage Services building is in the heart of downtown Nashville just two blocks north of Broadway. Just take Fourth Avenue northward two blocks to the intersection with Church Street. The building is on the northwest corner of Church and Fourth Avenue North. There is a historical marker in front of the building, but the marker references someone who has nothing to do with the building itself.

history

From 1859 until 1961, this building was the most famous and popular hotel in Nashville, called the Maxwell House Hotel.

A man named John Overton bid $15 for what he thought was a cow. To his surprise, he had actually bid on the lot on the corner of Fourth and Church. He began construction on the largest hotel in Nashville in 1859, using mostly slave labor. When Union forces occupied the city during the Civil War, the Union used the hotel as a prison for Confederate soldiers who were captured during the war. At one point during its life as a prison, the main stairway in the building collapsed, killing at least 37 Confederate prisoners of war. Closer to the end of the war, the building served as a Union army hospital. Countless Union soldiers died from their wounds within the building's walls.

After the war, Overton worked on finishing construction of the building. He named it the Maxwell House after his wife (whose maiden name was Maxwell). The hotel became quite popular as the 19th century was coming to a close, and over time some of the most famous people of the era stayed at the hotel. Seven presidents stayed here. Thomas Edison and Henry Ford also passed through the hotel at one time or another.

One day, when President Theodore Roosevelt stopped here, he was in the lobby drinking the hotel's own brand of coffee. As he finished his cup, he commented that it was "good to the last drop," inspiring one of the most famous advertising slogans of all time. While the hotel has been replaced by the SunTrust office building, Maxwell House remains one of the most popular brands of coffee in the country.

ghost story

Throughout the Maxwell House Hotel, before it was torn down to make room for office space, people would often encounter apparitions of Civil War soldiers, hear strange sounds, and see shadowy figures. When the new building was constructed on the site, these ghost stories essentially stopped. There is one ghost story, though, that still circulates at the new building which likely stems from the days when the hotel was still in commission.

In the main lobby of the SunTrust Mortgage Services building, people will see a woman descending the grand staircase. Several aspects of these sightings make them peculiar. First of all, the witnesses will see just the bottom half of the woman descending the staircase. Only her long, flowing dress is visible to the witnesses. The upper half of her body and her feet are never visible. What makes these sightings doubly strange is that the staircase itself is no longer there.

visiting

The ghost at the SunTrust Mortgage Services building is rather difficult to visit. Since the Maxwell House Hotel is long gone, the building is being used as office space by the SunTrust company. The lobby itself is accessible, so it is certainly possible to encounter the mysterious woman, but to access any part of the building past the lobby, you would need a special badge and would need to bypass security. Security will not allow you to simply stand in the lobby, especially if you explain that the reason you are there is to see a ghost descend a nonexistent stairwell.

TENNESSEE STATE CAPITOL

Capitol Hill, Nashville, TN 37243

directions

Very often considered the geographic center of Nashville, the Tennessee State Capitol is located high on Capitol Hill in downtown. Take Charlotte Avenue, and you'll find Capitol Hill between Sixth and Seventh avenues.

history

When, in the first half of the nineteenth century, Tennessee legislators decided they needed an appropriate structure in which to conduct state business, they put out a national call for an architect. William Strickland, a staunch northerner, was awarded the contract, and he faced fierce opposition from southern supporters. Amid local protests, Strickland moved to Nashville in 1845 with completed plans under his arm. In spite of the initial resistance, Tennesseans soon fell in love with his vision of the new capitol, and the cornerstone of the building was laid on July 4 of that year.

Bureaucratic squabbling frequently delayed construction over the next nine years, as did the continual depletion of funds. Also stalling the progress, though, was Samuel Morgan. Morgan had been hand-chosen by the Capitol Commission to keep Strickland on task and under budget, and he thought Strickland was prone to flights of fancy and cared little for the state's money issues. Strickland, on the other hand, viewed Morgan as a man who understood nothing about art.

While Morgan's unflinching determination slowed construction on the building, the state capitol slowly came to life. As Strickland's vision came nearer and nearer to completion, his health began to deteriorate. Convinced that the building would be the defining feature of his career, Strickland included designs for his own tomb within the building itself.

Although Strickland saw the capitol open for business in 1853, he didn't live to see it completed, dying on April 7, 1854. His son, Francis, completed the project for his father and witnessed the laying of the final stone on July 21, 1855.

Strickland was indeed interred in the tomb he designed for himself within the capitol building. In a cruel twist of fate, though, the State of Tennessee decided to reward Morgan's public service with the opportunity to be entombed within the capitol building. Morgan, Strickland's nemesis throughout the construction of the building, was laid to rest directly adjacent to Strickland.

ghost story

It seems that the rivalry between William Strickland and Samuel Morgan has continued to fester well after they both passed away. People will oftentimes hear the sounds of two men in the midst of a "spirited" argument. These sounds will echo throughout the halls of the colossal building. Most often, the arguments are heard within the hallways near the northern wall of the building. People usually attribute these phantom arguments to the ongoing debate between Strickland and Morgan over the completion of the capitol building.

These arguments frequently occur at night once the public has left the building. Capitol police and security guards will hear these arguments and will search the building extensively for the source of the sounds. The city police are occasionally called to aid them in their investigations, but the sources of these two male voices are never found.

Other ghostly activity here has a more direct effect on visitors to the historic building. Apparently the ghosts do not appreciate when anyone treats the building with any degree of disrespect, a behavior that would make sense if the ghosts were in fact the spirits of Strickland and Morgan. When tourists put their feet up on couches or benches in the building, a voice from an unseen source will ask that they remove their feet. People disrespecting the building in other ways will also be corrected by these phantom voices. It seems that despite their continuing arguments, both men still hold a reverent regard for the building they helped create.

visiting

The Tennessee State Capitol is open Monday–Friday from 9 a.m. to 4 p.m. Admission is free, and a brochure for a self-guided tour is available. Unfortunately, many of the ghostly arguments have been reported to happen at night, and since the building is still operating as the capitol of the state, it is completely closed to the public after 4 p.m. You stand the best chance of encountering these ghosts if they catch you inadvertently disrespecting the building. If you happen to do something that these ghostly builders do not like, you may just get a polite correction from one of them.

TENNESSEE STATE MUSEUM

505 Deaderick St., Nashville, TN 37243

directions

The Tennessee State Museum is in downtown Nashville on the north side of town near the Capitol building and St. Mary's Catholic Church. From Broadway, take Fifth Avenue North until you reach Deaderick Street. Turn left onto Deaderick Street, and you'll see the Tennessee State Museum there at the corner. Parking is located up and down the adjacent streets.

history

While the current building that houses the Tennessee State Museum wasn't built until 1981, the museum itself can trace its roots to 1817, when a portrait artist named Ralph E. W. Earl founded it. One of the oldest exhibits in the museum is a large portrait of Andrew Jackson, which has hung here from at least 1823.

The exhibit around which the hauntings take place dates back to the late 1850s. A man named Jeremiah Harris visited Egypt around that time and obtained a genuine 3,600-year-old Egyptian mummy. Harris brought the mummy back to Nashville in 1859, and in 1860, the Tennessee Historical Society gained possession of it. The mummy was proudly displayed in the State Capitol building. When Union forces took over the city, several Union soldiers decided that they would unwrap the mummy to search for jewels underneath the wrappings.

In 1937, the mummy found its way into the collection of the Tennessee State Museum. When the museum moved to its current location in 1981, the mummy moved with it. Apparently he doesn't like his new home.

ghost story

The stories of the hauntings at the Tennessee State Museum are highly unusual. According to some accounts, the night that the mummy was moved into the new building on Deaderick Street, it came to life and destroyed several important artifacts that were being displayed near it. And for the first several nights that it was there, it continued to come to life and destroy things throughout the building. A security guard was apparently so terrified of the mummy that he quit his job.

Stories have persisted throughout the years of the mummy sometimes coming to life. Tales of the mummy in more recent years are quite a bit tamer than the stories from 1981, though. More recently, people say that they have seen the mummy move slightly or that they saw a shadowy figure moving near the mummy exhibit. Gone are the days when the mummy would awaken at night and trash the building.

visiting

Entering the museum after closing time to see if the mummy is up and exploring the building is impossible. In order to see the living mummy, you will have to visit him during regular business hours. The museum is closed on Mondays and on major holidays. It's open on Tuesday through Saturday from 10 a.m. to 5 p.m., and on Sunday from 1 p.m. to 5 p.m. Admission is free. Every year around Halloween, a ghost story Festival called the "Haunted Museum" is held, during which you can enter an actual haunted museum and listen to ghost stories.

APPENDIX I:

Chapters Organized Geographically

DAVIDSON COUNTY

Downtown
Beer Sellar
Riverfront Tavern
The Melting Pot
Buffalo Billiards
Mulligan's Irish Pub
McFadden's Restaurant and Saloon
Hard Rock Cafe
Lawrence Record Shop
Ernest Tubb Record Shop
Printers Alley
Merchants Restaurant
Past Perfect
Fourth Avenue Parking Area / Alley
Robert's Western World
Tootsie's Orchid Lounge
Ryman Auditorium
Downtown Presbyterian Church
Nashville Public Library
Tennessee State Capitol
St. Mary's Catholic Church
Tennessee State Museum
SunTrust Mortgage Services
Hume-Fogg High School
Union Station Hotel
Flying Saucer

West of Downtown
Music Row
Dead Man's Curve at Demonbreun

Centennial Park
Dutchman's Curve
Old Tennessee State Prison

East of Downtown
Clover Bottom Mansion
Fort Negley
Old City Cemetery: Boulder Tombstone
Drake Motel
Pat's Hermitage Cafe
Mount Olivet Cemetery
Buchanan Log House
Two Rivers Parkway
Two Rivers Mansion
Two Rivers Golf Course
McNamara's Irish Pub

South of Downtown
Belmont Mansion
Shy's Hill
Belle Meade Plantation
Woodlawn Memorial Park Cemetery
Sunnyside Mansion
Grave of Granny White
Travellers Rest Plantation
Dillard's at The Mall at Green Hills
Edwin Warner Park

North of Downtown
Congress Inn
Opryland
Gaylord Opryland Resort and
    Convention Center

DAVIDSON COUNTY [CONT'D]
North of Downtown *(continued)*
Roy Acuff House
Grand Ole Opry House

Hermitage
McDonald's
The Hermitage

Donelson
Captain D's

ROBERTSON COUNTY
Adams
Adams Railroad Crossing
Bell Witch Cave

SUMNER COUNTY
Hendersonville
Rock Castle
Sanders Ferry Park
Old Beech Cemetery
Hendersonville Memory Gardens
Old Hendersonville Cemetery
Ellis Middle School

Gallatin
Palace Theater
Gallatin Town Square
Grecians Greek and Italian

Castalian Springs
Cragfont

Goodlettsville
Forest Lawn Memorial Gardens

WILSON COUNTY
Lebanon
Lebanon Premium Outlets
Cedar Grove Cemetery
Cumberland University
Cuz's Antiques Center

Mount Juliet
Fate Sanders Marina
Zierra Myst

RUTHERFORD COUNTY
Murfreesboro
Florence Road Railroad Crossing
Oaklands Historic House Museum
Evergreen Cemetery
Red Rose Coffee House and Bistro
    Building
Slaughter Pen at Stones River National
    Battlefield

Smyrna
Sam Davis Home

Rockvale
Dyer Cemetery

BEDFORD COUNTY
Wartrace
Walking Horse Hotel

MARSHALL COUNTY
Chapel Hill
Chapel Hill Ghost Lights

MAURY COUNTY

Columbia
Athenaeum Rectory

Mount Pleasant
Rattle and Snap Plantation

WILLIAMSON COUNTY

Franklin
Battle Ground Brewery & Restaurant
Lotz House
Carter House
Carnton Plantation
McGavock Confederate Cemetery

Spring Hill
Rippavilla Plantation

DICKSON COUNTY

White Bluff
White Screamer of White Bluff

CHEATHAM COUNTY

Ashland City
Blue Spring Cemetery

Joelton
Whites Creek Pike's Devil's Elbow

MONTGOMERY COUNTY

Clarksville
Austin Peay State University
Resthaven Memorial Gardens
Smith-Trahern Mansion

Palmyra
Wickham Stone Park

APPENDIX II:
Daytripping (or in this case, Nighttripping)

THE PARANORMAL PUB CRAWL
The best spirits in town

1st Stop: Riverfront Tavern

2nd Stop: Beer Sellar

3rd Stop: McFadden's Restaurant and Saloon

4th Stop: Hard Rock Cafe

5th Stop: Robert's Western World

6th Stop: Tootsie's Orchid Lounge

7th Stop: Flying Saucer

(Remember, do not drive drunk. This city has enough ghosts; we don't need you making any more.)

THE BATTLE OF FRANKLIN
Nashville's darkest night

1st Stop: Have a bite to eat at the Battle Ground Brewery across the river from the action.

2nd Stop: Approach the Lotz House, where the Lotzes took cover before fleeing to your next stop.

3rd Stop: Go to the Carter House, the epicenter of the battle.

4th Stop: Then follow the wounded to the Civil War hospital at Carnton Plantation.

5th Stop: And follow the dead to the McGavock Confederate Cemetery at Carnton.

OLD HANK WILLIAMS SR.
The most prolific ghost in Nashville

1st Stop: Search for old Hank wandering the streets of Music Row looking for a recording contract.

2ND STOP: Stop by Robert's Western World to find him, but if he's not there just go next door.

3RD STOP: Enjoy his favorite haunt, Tootsie's Orchid Lounge.

4TH STOP: Try to see him on stage at the Mother Church of Country Music, the Ryman Auditorium.

WEIRD NASHVILLE
Some of the strangest stories you'll ever hear

1ST STOP: See a bunch of headless statues in the middle of nowhere at Wickham Stone Park.

2ND STOP: Then stop by the Tennessee State Museum to see a mummy come to life.

3RD STOP: Explore Centennial Park, and see a plane with angel wings.

4TH STOP: Then head out to the strangest antiques shop in the world, Cuz's Antiques Center.

5TH STOP: Make your final stop in White Bluff to encounter the White Screamer, a child-eating llama.

MUSIC CITY UNDERGROUND
Sometimes what you see on the surface is a tiny fraction of the haunting

1ST STOP: Go to the basement of the Congress Inn, where the bodies may still be in the walls.

2ND STOP: Head downtown to the tunnels underneath Hume-Fogg High School.

3RD STOP: Follow those tunnels to the basement of Ernest Tubb Record Shop, which was once a morgue.

4TH STOP: Then go down to the Beer Sellar, a haunted bar by the river.

5TH STOP: Go north a little ways to the Bell Witch Cave.

APPENDIX III:

PARANORMAL INVESTIGATION GROUPS

AMERICAN PARANORMAL SOCIETY

Founded by a group of experienced paranormal investigators in 2003, the American Paranormal Society (APS) is an active group of individuals based in Nashville who share a few common goals: to investigate ghosts and hauntings, to offer paranormal education to the public, to assist others with spirit presences in their lives, and to further paranormal research as an acceptable scientific endeavor.

Should you need assistance with a spirit or haunting, please don't hesitate to contact this group. The APS is a non-profit organization, and its investigations are always free and confidential. It may be reached via the Internet at **www.apsociety. info** or via e-mail at info@apsociety.info.

TENNESSEE RESEARCH & INVESTIGATION OF PARANORMAL PHENOMENA

Tennessee Research & Investigation of Paranormal Phenomena (T.R.I.P.P.) was founded in 2009 by James and Misty Nash. James has more than 20 years' experience in paranormal investigations, and has participated in investigations at such locations as Sloss Furnaces in Birmingham, Alabama; Huntingdon College in Montgomery, Alabama; and Walking Horse Hotel in Wartrace, Tennessee. Misty has also participated in several investigations in and around Tennessee.

This group is dedicated to proving and documenting the existence of all things paranormal, not just ghosts and hauntings. Paranormal phenomena that T.R.I.P.P. investigates include, but are not limited to, ghosts, UFOs, and cryptozoology (Bigfoot, Loch Ness Monster, Jersey Devil, and so on). This is a non-profit organization that never charges for an investigation, as all information and evidence gathered are used for educational purposes.

T.R.I.P.P. is also affiliated with the American Paranormal Society, based in Nashville and founded by Donna Marsh. It has also extended a working relationship with other teams around the country. Reach this organization via its website, **trippghosthunters .webs.com,** and by e-mail at trippghosthunters@yahoo.com.

NASHVILLE GHOST AND PARANORMAL INVESTIGATORS

The Nashville Ghost and Paranormal Investigators (NGPI) are made up of Nashville-area residents from all walks of life with a common interest in the paranormal. They are committed to serving clients in a professional and confidential manner in accordance with their mission statement: to forward the study of the paranormal and to help both the living and those who have passed on. NGPI is committed to serve its clients with compassion, integrity, and professionalism through a balance of technology and experience in the field of the paranormal.

The team is led by a core group of individuals with more than 20 years of experience in the field of paranormal investigations. The group includes one medium and a sensitive.

Their goal for each investigation is quite simple. They will use their experience, technology, and collective energies to help those in need. This is not merely a group in search of electronic voice phenomena (EVPs) and photographic evidence. They wish to help those with a paranormal need to understand their situation and experiences. For more information, visit **www.ngpionline.com.**

TENNESSEE GHOSTHUNTERS

Established in 1997, Tennessee Ghosthunters was the first paranormal group to officially form in the state of Tennessee. They do not charge for an investigation, and they offer release forms if the client does not wish to have anything posted on the website. They have a large selection of equipment and very experienced investigators. The group's website, **www.tnghosthunters.com,** offers investigation requests, member info, and more, or you may contact founder Joanne Shelton at ersdjssls@comcast.net.

Shelton says that being a ghosthunter for 14 years has opened her eyes to death and the afterlife. Her group has conducted investigations in Tennessee, Alabama, Louisiana, and Kentucky, And they feel that they have collected enough evidence to convince even the biggest skeptic that ghosts do exist.

INNOVATIVE PARANORMAL RESEARCH

Do you believe in ghosts? Ever heard a noise or seen something you can't quite wrap your mind around? If so, you might want to give Nashville–based Innovative Paranormal Research (IPR) a call to see if they can help. This is an established, professional paranormal group whose main focus is taking care of their clients. IPR is a member of The Atlantic Paranormal Society (TAPS) family.

Ultimately, IPR's goal is to find answers and help others who have experienced paranormal activity but don't know what to do about it. Director Richard Edgeworth describes himself and his team members as humble, self-assured, and inquisitive as they search for answers, and they are comfortable with unsolved events. He warns that paranormal research is not for everyone—you can't be afraid of the dark or get stressed out easily. Also, you're going to walk through a lot of spider webs, so you'd better not be freaked out by them.

So, the next time you experience something you can't explain, remember that you're not alone. To contact IPR, visit **www.iprinvestigations.com** or call (615) 305-2055.

SOCIETY OF PARANORMAL INVESTIGATIONS & RESEARCH IN TENNESSEE

The Society of Paranormal Investigations & Research in Tennessee (SPIRIT) is based in Murfreesboro, Tennessee. This is a group of professional, working-class men and women dedicated to documenting and investigating hauntings and paranormal activity in Rutherford County and surrounding areas. They never charge for any services and will communicate and explain all findings in a timely manner.

Feel free to contact them for more information by visiting **www.spiritghostteam .com,** or e-mail contact@spiritghostteam.com.

GALLATIN PARANORMAL RESEARCH

Gallatin Paranormal Research (G.P.R.) was founded in late 2008 by Jason Hale. Always possessing an interest in the paranormal and finally having his first paranormal experience at the St. Augustine Lighthouse in Florida, Hale decided he wanted to get more involved in the paranormal field. After searching for weeks for a group he would fit into, Hale decided he didn't like the way many groups presented themselves and what they called evidence, so he started his own group. After putting an ad on Facebook, he was flooded with e-mails from people wanting to join. He narrowed the choices down to two people, Denise Brassel and Heather Dickey, and they started Gallatin Paranormal Research.

In their short time as a paranormal research group, G.P.R. has been lucky enough to investigate with some members of The Atlantic Paranormal Society (TAPS), and visit some of the most notorious haunted hot spots, such as Waverly Hills Sanatorium, St. Augustine Lighthouse, Pensacola Lighthouse, Fort Morgan, South Pittsburg Hospital, and many more.

G.P.R. prides itself on not being like every other team. They take a laid-back approach because they want clients to feel comfortable. G.P.R. is there to help and not just catch paranormal activity for themselves. They have been lucky so far with catching evidence for clients with their scientific approach to investigating. They do not use any type of metaphysical research. They are out for the proof, not the feeling. For more, check out their website, **www.gallatinparanormalresearch.com,** or call (615) 969-2925.

APPENDIX IV:

A HANDFUL OF HAUNTED LOCATIONS A
LITTLE MORE THAN AN HOUR AWAY

FORT DONELSON NATIONAL BATTLEFIELD

120 Fort Donelson Shores Rd. Dover, TN 37058

Fort Donelson sits about an hour and a half to the northwest of downtown Nashville, and it was one of the most important battlefields of the entire Civil War. Nashville served as an important commercial and supply center for the Confederacy, so the Confederate troops did their best to make sure that Nashville was well defended. Toward this goal, they built two large forts along the river to prevent any Union forces from using the river to take Nashville. The most impressive of these forts was Fort Donelson. The artillery batteries at the fort looked far down the river, and the fort utilized a natural depression in the landscape that made it militarily significant.

Despite the Confederacy's great advantages at Fort Donelson, Union forces were still able to take the fort with superior numbers and strategy. Once Donelson fell, the Confederates knew that the defense of Nashville would be impossible. Confederate forces abandoned the city, and Nashville was occupied by the Union throughout the rest of the war.

Fort Donelson itself plays host to its own share of paranormal activity, and tourists can gain access without charge during business hours. People near the battlefield after dark may hear the sounds of gunfire coming from the park. Others have actually seen soldiers in full Civil War uniforms walking around the park. These soldiers will be seen both during the day and at night. When the soldiers are approached, they mysteriously vanish as if they were never there in the first place.

FORT DONELSON NATIONAL CEMETERY

174 National Cemetery Rd., Dover, TN 37058

In 1867, Fort Donelson National Cemetery was created just adjacent to the battlefield for those soldiers who had died in the area during the Civil War. One of the men buried here is named Reuben Hammond, and he is the one who supposedly haunts this cemetery.

Reuben appears as a soldier, dressed in full uniform. He stands watch over the graves of the soldiers here, making sure that the final resting places of those who fell at

Fort Donelson are secure. Apparently, Reuben is rather lonely. If you do encounter the ghost of Reuben and you greet him cordially, he will follow you around the cemetery. If you manage to make a good impression with him, he will wave to you from the hill at the center of the cemetery as you leave the cemetery gates.

The cemetery has clearly posted hours. Make sure you don't enter outside of these hours. The best time to find Reuben is when no one else is in the cemetery. He appears more often when it is not busy.

DOVER HOTEL
101 Petty St., Dover, TN 37058

The Dover Hotel is also a part of the Fort Donelson National Battlefield but is across town from the battlefield and the national cemetery. The hotel is the location where the final surrender of the fort took place, so the building itself is important historically.

Ghostly activity at this hotel includes strange sounds inside and apparitions of Union soldiers in and around the building. Many times when the building is closed, tourists will walk up to the hotel and glance into the windows. Sometimes these tourists will spot a Civil War soldier in a blue uniform who suddenly vanishes.

MERIWETHER LEWIS NATIONAL PARK
Natchez Trace Parkway and Highway 20, Hohenwald, TN 38462

While most Americans are fully aware of Meriwether Lewis's importance in American history, most know little about his life after the fabled expedition in which he explored the expansive Louisiana Purchase. After his travels through the American West, he became the governor of the Northwest Territory. As governor, he soon ran into many financial difficulties and was forced to ask his friend Thomas Jefferson, President of the United States at the time, for federal funding.

Not willing to ask Jefferson for financial assistance through written correspondence, Lewis opted to visit the president in Washington to make his request. A leg of the journey took Lewis up the Natchez Trace, a trail that ran through Tennessee and ended near Nashville.

About 70 miles southwest of Nashville, Lewis stopped at a small inn called Grinder's Stand. This building still stands within the Meriwether Lewis National Park. According to the generally accepted history of that fateful night, Meriwether Lewis killed himself by shooting himself twice. There is debate about the circumstances surrounding his death, however. The gunshot wounds were to Lewis's chest and to the back of his head. This means that in order to kill himself, Lewis would have had to reload the weapon (not an easy feat in those days) and then somehow contort his body to put the gun to the back of his own head and pull the trigger; he would have had to do all of this while wounded from the initial gunshot to the chest.

Needless to say, though, Lewis is said to haunt the area in and around Grinder's Stand. People will see an apparition that looks exactly like Meriwether Lewis either in the area just outside of Grinder's Stand or actually inside the building, in the room where he supposedly committed suicide.

Lewis's family asked that the body, which is buried in the park, be exhumed for forensic analysis to prove once and for all whether the death was suicide or murder. In 2010, the National Park Service refused to exhume the body. Perhaps Lewis's ghost will continue to roam the park's grounds until the circumstances of his death are uncovered once and for all.

CRAZY GEORGE'S BRIDGE
Brotherton Mountain Road, Cookeville, TN 38506

In the small town of Cookeville, about an hour and a half from Nashville, there is a creepy bridge that is known to locals as Crazy George's Bridge. Many different stories abound about who Crazy George was in life. Some say that he was a drunk who would hang out and drink on the bridge. Others say that he was a railroad worker who would walk the railroad tracks that run under the bridge. The only common element to all the stories was that one day George somehow fell onto the tracks and was decapitated by a passing train.

Today, George seems to still look for his head. Legend goes that if you stop your car on the remote bridge and turn off the engine, the car will not restart. At this point, if you call for Crazy George three times, you will see a light appear on the railroad tracks. According to the legends, this is Crazy George himself, still searching for his missing head.

STAMPS CEMETERY
Brotherton Mountain Road/Woodcliff Road and Blaylock Mountain Road, Cookeville, TN 38506

Just a few miles from Crazy George's Bridge lies a decrepit and remote cemetery officially named Stamps Cemetery. More often, the locals call this cemetery the

Witch's Cemetery. The cemetery attained this strange name because of a single tombstone that sits within it. An image of a pentagram has been etched into the face of the grave marker.

According to legend, if someone were to touch the image of this pentagram exactly at the stroke of midnight, a demon will be released. This demon will haunt whoever touched the pentagram for the rest of his or her life.

While the cemetery does not have any posted signs warning that it closes at dark, exercise caution if you do find yourself here at midnight. Beyond the obvious danger of releasing a terrible demon into your life, solid proof exists that Satanic rituals have been performed here during the night. Small murdered animals and evidence of fire have been discovered in the cemetery the morning after such rituals.

HANNIWAL BRIDGE
Hannah Ward Bridge Road, Elkton, TN 38455

In the small town of Elkton, about an hour and a half from Nashville, there stands a 19th-century bridge that is no longer in use. According to legend, a mother and her infant child were once crossing the bridge in a horse-drawn carriage. Suddenly, an axle on the carriage broke as they were crossing, and mother and child were tossed helplessly off the bridge. Both mother and child were killed in the accident.

Today, echoes of this accident still exist at the bridge. If you listen closely late at night, you can hear what sounds like the distant cries of a baby. You don't have to listen as closely, however, to hear the terrified screams of a woman.

It is not easy to visit this bridge. The road that the bridge is on has very clearly marked "No Trespassing" signs and is gated.

GOLDEN HOLLOW ROAD
Golden Hollow Road, Kelso, TN 37348

About 1 hour and 45 minutes from Nashville in the town of Kelso, you'll find a haunted road called Golden Hollow Road. On a nice, crisp spring day in the early 1930s, two cars were headed in opposite directions on Golden Hollow Road. Going too fast to see one another in time, the two cars struck head-on, killing all seven people aboard the two cars.

The ghost on this road seems to show up more often during the springtime than in any other time of the year. When the flowers are starting to bloom and the cold of winter has begun to fade, people will sometimes see a group of several injured people limping down the side of the road. When these witnesses stop to help the victims, they simply vanish into thin air as if they were never there.

SCARCE CREEK BRIDGE
Lexington, TN 38351

About 1 hour and 45 minutes from Nashville spanning the Scarce Creek stands a creepy-looking bridge with an equally creepy history. A woman was walking across the bridge late one night when a car started speeding toward the bridge. Unwilling to stop to let the pedestrian cross, the car blared its horn three times, expecting her to move to the side. By the time the driver realized that she wasn't going to move, it was too late. The car hit the woman hard. Her neck snapped, and her head came off.

The driver of the car got out in panic, circling his vehicle five times and trying to figure out what to do. After circling the car the fifth time, he quickly jumped back in, rolled up the window, and drove away.

If you think that this sounds like an urban legend, you may be right. Here are the rules to follow in order to summon this particular ghost. You need to go to the bridge at midnight when there is a full moon. You must honk your horn three times on the bridge. You get out of your car and circle it five times, and then get back in and roll up your windows. If you manage to do all of this just right, the apparition of a headless woman will approach your car. Make sure you leave before she gets you.

APPENDIX V:

LOCATION CHECKLIST

LOCATION	Visited	Investigated	Found a Ghost
Adams Railroad Crossing			
Athenaeum Rectory			
Austin Peay State University			
Battle Ground Brewery & Restaurant			
Beer Sellar			
Bell Witch Cave			
Belle Meade Plantation			
Belmont Mansion			
Blue Spring Cemetery			
Buchanan Log House			
Buffalo Billiards			
Captain D's			
Carnton Plantation			
Carter House			
Cedar Grove Cemetery			
Centennial Park			
Chapel Hill Ghost Lights			
Clover Bottom Mansion			
Congress Inn			
Cragfont			
Cumberland University			
Cuz's Antiques Center			
Dead Man's Curve at Demonbreun			
Dillard's at The Mall at Green Hills			
Downtown Presbyterian Church			
Drake Motel			

LOCATION	Visited	Investigated	Found a Ghost
Dutchman's Curve			
Dyer Cemetery			
Edwin Warner Park			
Ellis Middle School			
Ernest Tubb Record Shop			
Evergreen Cemetery			
Fate Sanders Marina			
Florence Road Railroad Crossing			
Flying Saucer			
Forest Lawn Memorial Gardens			
Fort Negley			
Fourth Avenue Parking Area/Alley			
Gallatin Town Square			
Gaylord Opryland Resort and Convention Center			
Grave of Granny White			
Grecians Greek and Italian			
Hard Rock Cafe			
Hendersonville Memory Gardens			
The Hermitage			
Hume-Fogg High School			
Lawrence Record Shop			
Lebanon Premium Outlets			
Lotz House			
McDonald's			
McFadden's Restaurant and Saloon			
McGavock Confederate Cemetery			
McNamara's Irish Pub			
The Melting Pot			

LOCATION	Visited	Investigated	Found a Ghost
Merchants Restaurant			
Mount Olivet Cemetery			
Mulligan's Irish Pub			
Music Row			
Nashville Public Library			
Oaklands Historic House Museum			
Old Beech Cemetery			
Old City Cemetery: Boulder Tombstone			
Old Hendersonville Cemetery			
Old Tennessee State Prison			
Palace Theater			
Past Perfect			
Pat's Hermitage Cafe			
Printers Alley			
Rattle and Snap Plantation			
Red Rose Coffee House and Bistro Building			
Resthaven Memorial Gardens			
Rippavilla Plantation			
Riverfront Tavern			
Robert's Western World			
Rock Castle			
Roy Acuff House			
Ryman Auditorium			
St. Mary's Catholic Church			
Sam Davis Home			
Sanders Ferry Park			
Shy's Hill			

LOCATION	Visited	Investigated	Found a Ghost
Slaughter Pen at Stones River National Battlefield			
Smith-Trahern Mansion			
Sunnyside Mansion			
SunTrust Mortgage Services			
Tennessee State Capitol			
Tennessee State Museum			
Tootsie's Orchid Lounge			
Travellers Rest Plantation			
Two Rivers Golf Course			
Two Rivers Mansion			
Two Rivers Parkway			
Union Station Hotel			
Walking Horse Hotel			
White Screamer of White Bluff			
Whites Creek Pike's Devil's Elbow			
Wickham Stone Park			
Woodlawn Memorial Park Cemetery			
Zierra Myst			

ABOUT THE AUTHORS

DONNA MARSH

DONNA L. MARSH has always loved a good ghost story. Growing up in Maysville, Kentucky, she cleaned the local library out of every book she could find by the age of 10. When the family moved to her father's birthplace of Cookeville, Tennessee, in the mid-1970s, that love went with her. She found the library and started over on a new set of books.

A single mother, Marsh resides in Nashville with her younger son, a talented musician who plays nine instruments, and the Hounds of Hell, a weimaraner with ADHD and one diva of a Pembroke Welsh corgi. Her older son, a board-game enthusiast and self-proclaimed pop-culture guru, attends graduate school on the West Coast.

Marsh spends her days writing a column about ghosts and hauntings for **www .examiner.com** and her nights investigating them with the American Paranormal Society, a group she helped found in 2003.

JEFF MORRIS

THIS IS MORRIS'S THIRD BOOK. His first two, *Haunted Cincinnati and Southwest Ohio* and *Cincinnati Haunted Handbook*, were both about his hometown of Cincinnati, where he lives with his wife and two children. Morris founded a ghost tour in Miamitown, Ohio, in 2006 and still runs it to this day.

GARETT MERK

GARETT MERK is the founder
of the Tri-State Paranormal and
Oddities Observation Practitioners,
a paranormal study group based in
Cincinnati, Ohio. Having an interest in
ghosts since 2004, Merk has combined
his knowledge of science with his
passion for travel and technology to
learn about paranormal activities
around the world.